TRACING ONE WARM LINE
Poetry of Canada

Elisabeth Mouland, ed.

BREAKWATER

BREAKWATER
100 Water St.
P.O. Box 2188
St. John's, NF
A1E 6E6

Cover photo courtesy of Dennis Minty.

Canadian Cataloguing in Publication Data

Main entry under title:

Tracing one warm line

Educational ed.

Includes index.
ISBN 1-55081-089-8

1. Canadian poetry (English)   I. Mouland, Elisabeth
Anne, 1941-

PS8279.T722 1994	C811'.008	C94-950108-5
PR9195.25.T722 1994		

Reprinted 1999

DEDICATION

*To all the poets of Canada, many of whom are
unpublished and unsung.*

*To Carla Kean whose support, indomitable spirit
and love of poetry made the difference.*

"Ultimately, love and poetry and reason are the only things that can deal with any of the human perplexities. They're the only tools of consequence we have in any challenge."

Patrick Watson
ABILITIES, Summer '92

Of all the teachings we receive
this one is the most important:

Nothing belongs to you
of what there is,

of what you take,
you must share.

Chief Dan George

*Ah, for just one time, I would take The Northwest Passage
To find the hand of Franklin reaching for the Beaufort Sea
Tracing one warm line through a land so wide and savage
And make a Northwest Passage to the sea*

CONTENTS

The line begins . . .

A Selection of Aboriginal Voices

THE FATHER'S SONG

Great snowslide,
Stay away from my igloo,
I have my four children and my wife;
They can never enrich you.

Strong snowslide,
Roll past my weak house.
There sleep my dear ones in the world.
Snowslide, let their night be calm.

Sinister snowslide,
I just built an igloo here, sheltered from the
    wind.
It is my fault if it is put wrong.
Snowslide, hear me from your mountain.

Greedy snowslide,
There is enough to smash and smother.
Fall down over the ice,
Bury stones and cliffs and rocks.

Snowslide, I own so little in the world.
Keep away from my igloo, stop not our travels.
Nothing will you gain by our horror and death,
Mighty snowslide, mighty snowslide.

Little snowslide,
Four children and my wife are my whole
    world, all I owe,
All I can lose, nothing you can gain.
Snowslide, save my house, stay on your summit.

Inuit (Traditional)

HUNTING CARIBOU

I wriggle silently through the swamp,
my bow and arrow in my teeth.
The marsh is wide, the water icy cold.
There is nothing I can hide behind.

Crouching even lower,
quietly, I creep forward.
The caribou are grazing,
munching the juicy moss,
not thinking of me.
Until, suddenly
my arrow sinks deep
into the bull's side.

Startled, the herd
hastily scatters,
Heading for the hills
where they vanish.

This song about hunting was composed by an Iglulik living near Lyon Inlet.

KAYAK PADDLER'S SONG

When I'm out of the house in the open,
    I feel joy.
When I get out on the haphazard sea,
    I feel joy.
If it is really fine weather,
    I feel joy.
If the sky really clears nicely,
    I feel joy.
May it continue thus
    for the good of my sealing!
May it continue thus
    for the good of my hunting!
May it continue thus
    for the good of my singing-match!
May it continue thus
    for the good of my drum-song!

An Inuit work song.

WAR CHANT

Young men, help me, do help me!
I love my country so.
That is why I am fighting.

Most Plains Indians thought of their land extending as far as the buffalo roamed and the imaginary line created by the settlers between Canada and the United States made very little sense to them. At home on either side of the border, they were as likely to consider themselves Canadians as Americans, if they ever thought of themselves as either.

HUNGER

Fear hung over me.
I dared not try
to hold out in my hut.

Hungry and chilled,
I stumbled inland,
tripping, falling constantly.

At Little Musk Ox Lake
the trout made fun of me;
they wouldn't bite.

On I crawled,
and reached the Young Man's River
where I caught salmon once.

I prayed
for fish or reindeer
swimming in the lake.

My thought
reeled into nothingness
like run-out fishing line.

This song, which is very old, was learned early this century by Knut Ras-
mussen, a Danish explorer, from Kingmerut, a Copper Eskimo from Ellis River.
The translation here is from Eskimo Poems *by Tom Lowenstein.*

SONG TO THE WANDERER

I cannot stay, I cannot stay!
I must take my canoe and fight the waves,
For the Wanderer spirit is seeking me.

The beating of great, black wings on the sun,
The Raven has stolen the ball of the sun,
From the Kingdom of Light he has stolen the sun.

I cannot stay, I cannot stay!
The Raven has stolen the child of the Chief,
Of the Highest Chief in the Kingdom of Light.

The Slave Wife born from the first clam shell
Is in love with the boy who was stolen away,
The lovers have taken the Raven's fire.

The Slave who was born from the first clam shell
Has made love to the wife who was born from the shell,
This Slave man has stolen her treasures away.

He is the Wanderer spirit who calls me,
He is the One who has charge of the birds,
He is the One who loves plants, beasts, and fish.

I am the one who loves the wild woods,
I am the one who embraces the sea.
I must take my canoe and escape tonight!

Traditional Haida* Indian Poem
(Translated by Hermia Harris Fraser)

* *"Haida" is the popular name for the Skittagetan Indians*
of Queen Charlotte Islands, British Columbia.

THE SONG MY PADDLE SINGS

West wind, blow from your prairie nest,
Blow from the mountains, blow from the west.
The sail is idle, the sailor too;
O! wind of the west, we wait for you.
    Blow, Blow!
    I have wooed you so,
  But never a favour you bestow.
You rock your cradle the hills between,
But scorn to notice my white lateen.

I stow the sail, unship the mast:
I wooed you long, but my wooing's past;
My paddle will lull you into rest.
O! drowsy wind of the drowsy west,
    Sleep, sleep,
    By your mountain steep,
  Or down where the prairie grasses sweep!
Now fold in slumber your laggard wings,
For soft is the song my paddle sings.

August is laughing across the sky,
Laughing while paddle, canoe and I,
    Drift, drift,
    Where the hills uplift
  On either side of the current swift.

The river rolls in its rocky bed;
My paddle is plying its way ahead;
    Dip, dip,
    While the waters flip
  In foam as over their breast we slip.

And oh, the river runs swifter now;
The eddies circle about my bow.
    Swirl, swirl!
    How the ripples curl
  In many a dangerous pool awhirl!

And forward far the rapids roar,
Fretting their margin for evermore.
   Dash, dash,
    With a mighty crash,
  They seethe, and boil, and bound, and splash.

Be strong, O paddle! be brave, canoe!
The reckless waves you must plunge into.
   Reel, reel,
    On your trembling keel,
  But never a fear my craft will feel.

We've raced the rapid, we're far ahead!
The river slips through its silent bed.
   Sway, sway,
    As the bubbles spray
  And fall in tinkling tunes away.

And up on the hills against the sky,
A fir tree rocking its lullaby,
   Swings, swings,
    Its emerald wings,
  Swelling the song that my paddle sings.

               E. Pauline Johnson

And the line continues...

Of Explorers, Voyageurs, and Adventurers

EXPLORER

Gone. Not one that asked which way was north.
What does it mean the south inverted so?
And some never spoke, gathering notes
in little books, rushing up the rivers,
away, their eyes open everywhere,
huge as lakes, no thing, no

hill, no emptiness boyond
that was not there reflected—flat, reversed
and floating past: so are Kelsey's eyes,
rhyming *fate* with *late*, to see his shade
always farther ahead and entering trees
days before he enters his notes, to see

fate, arrive and find it gone, always
too late, sight rhymes for a fiction un-
seen. Or other eyes, La Vérendrye's,
seizing the syllables of trees in French
where they speak, edging the wide shores with green
words, outlines falling apart at summer's end.

They are all—MacKenzie, Henry, Jacques Cartier—
maps of eyes, how many miles of degrees
falling cleanly through them, outsides marked
and put away, lakes whose surface lies
soundless, other, and all that's mirrored there
is wet—trees, canoes, hills and sky—

dripping from fingers moving away from south,
lattitudes drownung wherever you take the world
in. Why do you ever come back, your backs turned,
gazing dully through strata and degrees,
to tell us, as Rupert Brooke would one day say:
"A godless place. And the dead do not return"?

How shall we sing the godless, the not yet
dead? O name the long measure of the world
where outlines lie before us on a page,
black notes against the white surveyed—
as one might turn north to music scored
for flutes, to rhyme *death* with *breath*, the air

figuring itself, proleptic and sure,
going always into itself, without
edges, no shade but lenghts of light
refracted and still. Other music, the trees
transmitted to a speech of gods we cannot hear,
unwritten, grace notes without design.

E. D. Blodgett

JACQUES CARTIER

In the seaport of Saint Malo 'twas a smiling morn in May,
When the Commodore Jacques Cartier to the westward sailed away;
In the crowded old Cathedral all the town were on their knees
For the safe return of kinsmen from the undiscovered seas;
And every autumn blast that swept o'er pinnacle and pier
Filled manly hearts with sorrow, and gentle hearts with fear.

A year passed o'er Saint Malo—again came round the day,
When the Commodore Jacques Cartier to the westward sailed away;
But no tidings from the absent had come the way they went,
And tearful were the vigils that many a maiden spent;
And manly hearts were filled with gloom, and gentle hearts with fear,
When no tidings came from Cartier at the closing of the year.

But the earth is as the Future, it hath its hidden side,
And the Captain of Saint Malo was rejoicing in his pride
In the forests of the North—while his townsmen mourned his loss,
He was rearing on Mount-Royal the fleur-de-lis and cross;
And when two months were over and added to the year,
Saint Malo hailed him home again, cheer answering to cheer.

He told them of a region, hard, ironbound, and cold,
Where no seas of pearl abounded, nor mines of shining gold,
Where the wind from Thulé freezes the word upon the lip,
And the ice in spring comes sailing athwart the early ship;
He told them of the frozen scene until they thrill'd with fear,
And piled fresh fuel on the hearth to make them better cheer.

But when he changed the strain—he told how soon are cast
In early Spring the fetters that hold the waters fast;
How the Winter causeway broken is drifted out to sea,
And rills and rivers sing with pride the anthem of the free;
How the magic wand of Summer clad the landscape to his eyes,
Like the dry bones of the just when they wake in Paradise.

He told them of the Algonquin braves—the hunters of the wild;
Of how the Indian mother in the forest rocks her child;
Of how, poor souls, they fancy in every living thing
A spirit good or evil, that claims their worshipping;
Of how they brought their sick and maim'd for him to breathe upon,
And of the wonders wrought for them through the Gospel of
    St. John.

He told them of the river, whose mighty current gave
Its freshness for a hundred leagues to ocean's briny wave;
He told them of the glorious scene presented to his sight,
What time he reared the cross and crown on Hochelaga's height,
And of the fortess cliff that keeps of Canada the key,
And they welcomecd back Jacques Cartier from his perils o'er the
    sea.

Thomas d'Arcy McGee

CHANSON DES VOYAGEURS

Dans le cours du voyage,
Expose aux naufrages;
Le corps trempé dans l'eau,
Éveillé par les oiseaux;
Nous n'avons de repos
Ni le jour ni la nuit.
N'y a que de l'ennui,
Préoccupé du temps,
Battu par les vents...

Ah! J'vous dis, mes frères
'Y a personne sur terre
Qu' endur' tant de misère.
Qui, c'est un marriage
Que d'epouser le voyage.
Moi j'attends la journée,
Jour de mon arrivée!
Jamais plus je n'irai
Dans ces pays damnés
Pour tant m'y ennuyer.

Anonymous

SONG OF THE VOYAGEURS

In the course of the journey,
Subject to sudden mishaps,
Your body soaked to the bone,
Woken before dawn by the birds;
With no rest,
neither night nor day,
With nothing but wearisome work,
Always worrying about the approach of winter
and being beaten by the winds...

Oh! I tell you, comrades,
There is no one on earth
Who endures as much misery as we do
who are married to our work.
As for me, I can't wait
until we get home again.
Never again will I come
to this damned country
which has almost worn me out.

A romantic myth has grown up around the voyageurs, those hardy canoemen who often paddled half way across the continent in search of beaver pelts. Most of the voyageurs were forced by economic necessity into what was a hard, dirty and poorly paid job. For a realistic picture of what life in the woods was like, we only have to look at the songs composed and sung by the voyageurs as they paddled along the northern lakes and rivers.

I AM A FALLEN SON

A fallen son of a breed superhuman,
A violent, risk-taking, muscular race,
I long for virgin lands as did they in their place
When September brings the drab grey days again.

All the brutal past of these *coureurs des bois* —
Hunters, trappers, sawyers, raftsmen on stages,
Merchants, adventurers, workers for wages —
Calls me on a five-month flight to lands that are raw.

I dream of going as my ancestors went;
I hear in me the cry of the wide, white plains
That they ran over, haloed in hurricanes,
And like them I hate a master's constraint.

And when a bitter storm on their backs was laid,
They cursed the valley and they cursed the plain,
They cursed the wool-robbing wolves with might and main,
Their curses made their bad luck seem less bad.

When in thought their far-off wives they saw again
And the landscape swam before them in dim waves,
They dried their eyes on the backs of their sleeves
And their wide mouths sang, "*À la claire fontaine...*"

So oft to forest echoes I have heard
This song repeated, so well the air I know
Which the nigtingale sings on the topmost bough,
That my secret thoughts are mingled with the bird.

Whether I bend beneath an unseen wrench
In the sharp hubbub of a sad farewell,
Whether before obstacle or tie, I feel
The tingling shiver which made their huge fists clench;

Whether from those who have not known despair,
Who died in their dreams of conquering nature,
I inherit this wild taste for adventure
Which sometimes at night engulfs me everywhere;

Through our barren years I am like the beech tree
Whose sap dried up although its foliage stayed,
And it is of dead desires that my leaves are made
When I dream of being like my ancestry;

But the indistinct words that stick in my craw
Are still these: a rosebush, a sprig, a green spray,
An oak, a nightingale in the leaves of day,
And, as in the days of my ancestral *coureurs des bois,*

The landscape sings either my grief or my joy.

Alfred DesRochers
(Translated by Fred Cogswell)

PROSPECTOR

Old man you prospected summer
country of caves and gold.
With the rattlesnake and spider
you were a black widow without a mate
gone deep chrome yellow.
You shared with the sun
a babble of flowers and full
brown flawless centers where
you walked in a wilderness
of golden sleep.

Once I was a child
and saw you touch a mountain
wasp with your finger
tip to wing he didn't move
but shivered gently his petal shells
of yellow and black in the wide corner
of August. You watched solitary
wasps float down sunflower fields.

Old man I dreamed you
wandered the mountains
in spring and planted
the hills with golden flowers.
When they found you
they said you were dead
but I knew that the wasps
had planted their eggs in you
and flowers were growing
out of your sleeping eyes.

Patrick Lane

A Selection of Canadian Classics

THE FORSAKEN

I
Once in the winter
Out on a lake
In the heart of the north-land,
Far from the Fort
And far from the hunters,
A Chippewa woman
With her sick baby,
Crouched in the last hours
Of a great storm.
Frozen and hungry,
She fished through the ice
With a line of the twisted
Bark of the cedar,
And a rabbit-bone hook
Polished and barbed;
Fished with the bare hook
All through the wild day,
Fished and caught nothing;
While the young chieftain
Tugged at her breasts,
Or slept in the lacings
Of the warm *tikanagan*.
All the lake-surface
Streamed with the hissing
Of millions of iceflakes
Hurled by the wind;
Behind her the round
Of a lonely island
Roared like a fire
With the voice of the storm
In the deeps of the cedars.
Valiant, unshaken,
She took of her own flesh,
Baited the fish-hook
Drew in a gray-trout,
Drew in his fellows,
Heaped them beside her,
Dead in the snow.
Valiant, unshaken,

She faced the long distance,
Wolf-haunted and lonely,
Sure of her goal
And the life of her dear one:
Tramped for two days,
On the third in the morning,
Saw the strong bulk
Of the Fort by the river,
Saw the wood-smoke
Hang soft in the spruces,
Heard the keen yelp
Of the ravenous huskies
Fighting for whitefish:
Then she had rest.

II
Years and years after,
When she was old and withered,
When her son was an old man
And his children filled with vigour,
They came in their northern tour on the verge of winter,
To an island in a lonely lake.
There one night they camped, and on the morrow
Gathered ther kettles and birch-bark
Their rabbit-skin robes and their mink-traps,
Launched their canoes and slunk away through the islands,
Left her alone forever,
Without a word of farewell,
Because she was old and useless,
Like a paddle broken and warped,
Or a pole that was splintered.
Then, without a sigh,
Valiant, unshaken,
She smoothed her dark locks under her kerchief,
Composed her shawl in state,
Then folded her hands ridged with sinews and corded with veins,
Folded them across her breasts spent with the nourishing of
    children,
Gazed at the sky past the tops of the cedars,
Saw two spangled nights arise out of the twilight,
Saw two days go by filled with the tranquil sunshine,
Saw, without pain, or dread, or even a moment of longing:

Then on the third great night there came thronging and thronging
Millions of snowflakes out of a windless cloud;
They covered her close with a beautiful crystal shroud,
Covered her deep and silent.
But in the frost of the dawn,
Up from the life below
Rose a column of breath
Through a tiny cleft in the snow,
Fragile, delicately drawn,
Wavering with its own weakness,
In the wilderness a sign of the spirit,
Persisting still in the sight of the sun
Till day was done.
Then all light was gathered up by the hand of God and hid in His
    breast,
Then there was born a silence deeper than silence,
Then she had rest.

Duncan Campbell Scott

ON THE WAY TO THE MISSION

They dogged him all one afternoon,
Through the bright snow,
Two whitemen servants of greed;
He knew that they were there,
But he turned not his head;
He was an Indian trapper;
He planted his snow-shoes firmly,
He dragged the long toboggan
Without rest.

The three figures drifted
Like shadows in the mind of a seer;
The snow-shoes were whisperers
On the threshold of awe;
The toboggan made the sound of wings,
A wood-pigeon sloping to her nest.

The Indian's face was calm.
He strode with the sorrow of fore-knowledge,
But his eyes were jewels of content
Set in circles of peace.

They would have shot him;
But momently in the deep forest,
They saw something flit by his side;
Their hearts stopped with fear.
Then the moon rose.
They would have left him to the spirit,
But they saw the long toboggon
Rounded well with furs,
With many a silver fox-skin,
With the pelts of mink and of otter.

They were the servants of greed;
When the moon grew brighter
And the spruces were dark with sleep,
They shot him.
When he fell on a shield of moonlight
One of his arms clung to his burden;
The snow was not melted:
The spirit passed away.

Then the servants of greed
Tore off the cover to count their gains;
They shuddered away into the shadows,
Hearing each the loud heart of the other.
Silence was born.

There in the tender moonlight,
  As sweet as they were in life,
Glimmered the ivory features,
  Of the Indian's wife.

In the manner of Montagnais women
  Her hair was rolled with braid;
Under her waxen fingers
  A crucifux was laid.

He was drawing her down to the Mission,
  To bury her there in spring,
When the bloodroot comes and the windflower
  To silver everything.

But as a gift of plunder
  Side by side were they laid,
The moon went on to her setting
  And covered them with shade.

Duncan Campbell Scott

CANADIAN RAILROAD TRILOGY

There was a time in this fair land when the railroad did not run,
When the wild majestic mountains stood alone against the sun,
Long before the white man and long before the wheel
When the green dark forest was too silent to be real.

But time has no beginnings and history has no bounds,
As to this verdant country they came from all around,
They sailed upon her waterways and they walked the forests tall,
Built the mines, the mills and the factories for the good of us all.

And when the young man's fancy was turnin' in the spring,
The railroad men grew restless for to hear the hammers ring,
Their minds were overflowin' with the visions of their day
And many a fortune won and lost and many a debt to pay.

For they looked in the future and what did they see,
They saw an iron road runnin' from the sea to the sea,
Bringin' the goods to a young, growin' land
All up from the seaports and into their hands.
"Look away!", said they, "across this mighty land,
From the eastern shore to the western strand!"

"Bring in the workers and bring up the rails,
We gotta lay down the tracks and tear up the trails,
Open her heart, let the life blood flow,
Gotta get on our way 'cause we're movin' too slow
Get on our way 'cause we're movin' too slow."

"Behind the blue rockies the sun is declinin',
The stars they come stealin' at the close of the day,
Across the wide prairie our loved ones lie sleeping
Beyond the dark ocean in a place far away."

"We are the navvies who work upon the railway,
Swingin' our hammers in the bright blazin' sun,
Livin' on stew and drinkin' bad whiskey,
Bendin' our backs 'til the long days are done."

"We are the navvies who work upon the railway,
Swingin' our hammers in the bright blazin' sun,
Layin' down track and buildin' the bridges,
Bendin' our backs 'till the railroad is done."

"So over the mountains and over the plains,
Into the muskeg and into the rain,
Up the Saint Lawrence all the way to Gaspé,
Swingin' our hammers and drawin' our pay,
Layin' 'em in and tyin' 'em down,
Away to the bunkhouse and into the town,
A dollar a day and a place for my head
A drink to the living, a toast to the dead!"

"Oh, the song of the future has been sung,
All the battles have been won,
On the mountain tops we stand,
All the world at our command.
We have opened up the soil
With our teardrops—
And our toil."

For there was a time in this fair land when the railroad did not run,
When the wild majestic mountains stood alone against the sun,
Long before the white man and long before the wheel,
When the green dark forest was too silent to be real
When the green dark forest was too silent to be real.
And many are the dead men,
Too silent
To be real.

Gordon Lightfoot

THE SPELL OF THE YUKON

I wanted the gold, and I sought it;
  I scrabbled and mucked like a slave.
Was it famine or scurvy — I fought it;
  I hurled my youth into a grave.
I wanted the gold, and I got it —
  Came out with a fortune last fall, —
Yet somehow life's not what I thought it,
  And somehow the gold isn't all.

No! There's the land. (Have you seen it?)
  It's the cussedest land that I know,
From the big, dizzy mountains that screen it
  To the deep, deathlike valleys below.
Some say God was tired when He made it;
  Some say it's a fine land to shun;
Maybe; but there's some as would trade it
  For no land on earth — and I'm one.

You come to get rich (damned good reason);
  You feel like an exile at first;
You hate it like hell for a season,
  And then you are worse than the worst.
It grips you like some kinds of sinning;
  It twists you from foe to a friend;
It seems it's been since the beginning;
  It seems it will be to the end.

I've stood in some mighty-mouthed hollow
  That's plumb-full of hush to the brim;
I've watched the big, husky sun wallow
  In crimson and gold, and grow dim,
Till the moon set the pearly peaks gleaming,
  And the stars tumbled out, neck and crop;
And I've thought that I surely was dreaming,
  With the peace o' the world piled on top.

The summer — no sweeter was ever;
  The sunshiny woods all athrill;
The grayling aleap in the river,
  The bighorn asleep on the hill.
The strong life that never knows harness;
  The wilds where the caribou call;
The freshness, the freedom, the farness —
  O God! how I'm stuck on it all.

The winter! the brightness that blinds you,
  The white land locked tight as a drum,
The cold fear that follows and finds you,
  The silence that bludgeons you dumb.
The snows that are older than history,
  The woods where the weird shadows slant;
The stillness, the moonlight, the mystery,
  I've bade 'em good-by — but I can't.

There's a land where the mountains are nameless,
  And the rivers all run God knows where;
There are lives that are erring and aimless,
  And deaths that just hang by a hair;
There are hardships that nobody reckons;
  There are valleys unpeopled and still;
There's a land — oh, it beckons and beckons
  And I want to go back — and I will.

They're making my money diminish;
  I'm sick of the taste of champagne.
Thank God! when I'm skinned to a finish
  I'll pike to the Yukon again.
I'll fight — and you bet it's no sham-fight;
  It's hell! — but I've been there before;
And it's better than this by a damsite —
  So me for the Yukon once more.

There's gold, and it's haunting and haunting;
  It's luring me on as of old;
Yet it isn't the gold that I'm wanting
  So much as just finding the gold.
It's the great, big broad land 'way up yonder,
  It's the forests where silence has lease;
It's the beauty that thrills me with wonder,
  It's the stillness that fills me with peace.

Robert Service

THE DARK STAG

A startled stag, the blue-grey Night,
  Leaps down beyond black pines.
Behind—a length of yellow light—
  The hunter's arrow shines:
His moccasins are stained with red,
  He bends upon his knee,
From covering peaks his shafts are sped,
The blue mists plume his mighty head,—
  Well may the swift Night flee!

The pale, pale Moon, a snow-white doe,
  Bounds by his dappled flank:
They beat the stars down as they go,
  Like wood-bells growing rank.
The winds lift dewlaps from the ground,
  Leap from the quaking reeds;
Their hoarse bays shake the forests round,
With keen cries on the track they bound,—
  Swift, swift the dark stag speeds!

Away! his white doe, far behind,
  Lies wounded on the plain;
Yells at his flank the nimblest wind,
  His large tears fall in rain;
Like lily-pads, small clouds grow white
  About his darkling way;
From his bald nest upon the height
The red-eyed eagle sees his flight;
He falters, turns, the antlered Night,—
  The dark stag stands at bay!

His feet are in the waves of space;
  His antlers broad and dun
He lowers he turns his velvet face
  To front the hunter, Sun;
He stamps the lilied clouds, and high
  His branches fill the west.
The lean stork sails across the sky,
The shy loon shrieks to see him die,
  The winds leap at this breast.

Roar the rent lakes as thro' the wave
   Their silver warriors plunge,
As vaults from core of crystal cave
   The strong, fierce muskallunge;
Red torches of the sumach glare,
   Fall's council-fires are lit;
The bittern, squaw-like, scolds the air;
The wild duck splashes loudly where
The rustling rice-spears knit.

Shaft after shaft the red Sun speeds:
   Rent the stag's dappled side,
His breast, fanged by the shrill winds, bleeds,
He staggers on the tide;
He feels the hungry waves of space
   Rush at him high and blue;
Their white spray smites his dusky face,
Swifter the Sun's fierce arrows race
   And pierce his stout heart thro'.

His antlers fall; once more he spurns
   The hoarse hounds of the day;
His blood upon the crisp blue burns,
   Reddens the mounting spray;
His branches smite the wave—with cries
   The loud winds pause and flag—
He sinks in space—red glow the skies,
The brown earth crimsons as he dies,
   The strong and dusky stag.

              Isabella Valancy Crawford

LOW TIDE ON GRAND PRÉ

The sun goes down, and over all
    These barren reaches by the tide
Such unelusive glories fall,
    I almost dream they yet will bide
    Until the coming of the tide.

And yet I know that not for us,
    By any ecstasy of dream,
He lingers to keep luminous
    A little while the grievous stream,
    Which frets, uncomforted of dream—

A grievous stream, that to and fro
    Athrough the fields of Acadie
Goes wandering, as if to know
    Why one beloved face should be
    So long from home and Acadie.

Was it a year or lives ago
    We took the grasses in our hands,
And caught the summer flying low
    Over the waving meadow lands,
    And held it there between our hands?

The while the river at our feet—
    A drowsy inland meadow stream—
At set of sun the after-heat
    Made running gold, and in the gleam
    We freed our birch upon the stream.

There down along the elms at dusk
    We lifted dripping blade to drift,
Through twilight scented fine like musk,
    Where night and gloom awhile uplift,
    Nor sunder soul and soul adrift.

And that we took into our hands
    Spirit of life or subtler thing—
Breathed on us there, and loosed the bands
    Of death, and taught us, whispering,
    The secret of some wonder-thing.

Then all your face grew light, and seemed
    To hold the shadow of the sun;
The evening faltered, and I deemed
    That time was ripe, and years had done
    Their wheeling underneath the sun.

So all desire and all regret,
    And fear and memory, were naught;
One to remember or forget
    The keen delight our hands had caught;
    Morrow and yesterday were naught.

The night was fallen, and the tide...
    Now and again comes drifting home,
Across these aching barrens wide,
    A sigh like driven wind or foam:
    In grief the flood is bursting home.

                        Bliss Carman

SAGA OF THE SHIELD

The Indian sits silent
    and smokes the calumet
    thinking only
    of what he had looked upon...

Successive native groups
    once wandered here
Most recently Ojibway ruled
    this great lone land
    of primeval savagery
    entrenched
    in Nature's rock-fringed lakes
    and rapid rivers
    midst miles of muskeg
    and thickly tangled trees
Where D.C. Scott immortalized the
    "ululating laughter of the loon"
    that mocked
    the white man's
    premature intrusion
    into this height of land
    where Indian
    lived common-law with Nature.
Ambassadors arrived on rival errands—
    the black robe saving souls
    and traders seeking furs.
Fleming mapped an iron road
    and pierced the lonely land
    with people trains
    bringing loggers
    toting chains
    prospectors
    staking claims.

Soon silent skies were filled
    with shrill staccato drills
    and nitroglycerine
    tore at the Shield's tough skin
    in search
    of mineral wealth.
Today's scarred surface
    bears mute testimony
    to the Shield's surrender.

Only the Indian sits silent
    and smokes the calumet
    thinking of what
    he has looked upon.

Betty L.Dyck

TRANS CANADA

Pulled from our ruts by the made-to-order gale
We sprang upward into a wider prairie
And dropped Regina below like a pile of bones.

Sky tumbled upon us in waterfalls,
But we were smarter than a Skeena salmon
And shot our silver body over the lip of air
To rest in a pool of space
On the top storey of our adventure.

A solar peace
And a six-way choice.

Clouds, now, are the solid substance,
A floor of wool roughed by the wind
Standing in waves that halt in their fall.
A still of troughs.

The plane, our planet,
Travels on roads are not seen or laid
But sound in instruments on pilots' ears,

While underneath
The sure wings
Are the everlasting arms of science.

Man, the lofty worm, tunnels his latest clay,
And bores his new career.

This frontier, too, is ours.
This everywhere whose life can only be led
At the pace of a rocket
Is common to man and man,
And every country below is an I land.

The sun sets on its top shelf,
And stars seem father from our nearer grasp.

I have sat by night beside a cold lake
And touched things smoother than moonlight on still water,
But the moon on this cloud sea is not human,
And here is no shore, no intimacy,
Only the start of space, the road to suns.

                              F.R. Scott

BONNE ENTENTE

The advantages of living with two cultures
Strike one at every turn,
Especially when one finds a notice in an office building:
'This elevator will not run on Ascension Day';
Or reads in the *Montreal Star*:
'Tomorrow being the Feast of the Immaculate Conception,
There will be no collection of garbage in the city';
Or sees on the restaurant menu the bilingual dish:

DEEP APPLE PIE
TARTE AUX POMMES PROFONDES

F.R. Scott

ICE

When Winter scourged the meadow and the hill
And in the withered leafage worked his will,
The water shrank, and shuddered, and stood still, —
Then built himself a magic house of glass,
Irised with memories of flowers and grass,
Wherein to sit and watch the fury pass.

Charles G.D. Roberts

MORNING ON THE LIÈVRE

Far above us where a jay
Screams his matins to the day,
Capped with gold and amethyst,
Like a vapour from the forge
Of a giant somewhere hid
Out of hearing of the clang
Of his hammer, skirts of mist
Slowly up the woody gorge
Lift and hang.

Softly as a cloud we go,
Sky above and sky below,
Down the river; and the dip
Of the paddles scarcely breaks,
With the little silvery drip
Of the water as it shakes
From the blades, the crystal deep
Of the silence of the morn,
Of the forest yet asleep;

And the river reaches borne
In a mirror, purple gray,
Sheer away
To the misty line of light,
Where the forest and the stream
In the shadow meet and plight,
Like a dream.

From amid a stretch of reeds,
Where the lazy river sucks
All the water as it bleeds
From a little curling creek,
And the muskrats peer and sneak
In around the sunken wrecks
Of a tree that swept the skies
Long ago,
On a sudden seven ducks
With a splashy rustle rise,
Stretching out their seven necks,
One before, and two behind,
And the others all arow,
And as steady as the wind
With a swivelling whistle go,
Through the purple shadow led,
Til we only hear their whir
In behind a rocky spur,
Just ahead.

Archibald Lampman

*Lièvre—The Lièvre is a tributary of the Ottawa River, joining it east of the
capital. It was just one of the many waterways in Ontario and Quebec explored on
canoe trips by Lampman and his fellow poet, Duncan Campbell Scott.*

FISH

A fish dripping
sparkling drops
of crystal water,
pulled from the lake;
long has it dwelt
in the cool water,
in the cold water
of the lake.

Long has it wandered
to and fro
over the bottom
of the lake
among mysterious
recesses
there in the semi-
light of the water;

now to appear
surprised, aghast,
out of its element
into the day; —
out of the cold
and shining lake
the fish dripping
sparkling water.

W.W.E. Ross

TOM THOMSON

It was a grey day
with a drizzle of rain,
something of fey
in the air
as though the lake,
the islands,
the sky
were watching,
waiting,
waiting for what?
A sense of doom
in the air
with silence everywhere
as though a god
had spoken,
and then a loon laughed
and the spell was broken,
the spell was broken.

And Tom Thomson laughed
and his friends laughed
as he launched his canoe
from the dock
and paddled away
with his lures and his lines
to befool the old trout
they had lost so often
in the bay in the river
below Joe Lake Dam;
and he turned
with a wave of his hand
and was gone.

And a loon laughed
and the old trout
waited in the bay
and the sky and lake watched
but he never came
was never seen again
till his body floated
on the surface
eight days later.

What happened?
No one knows,
no one will ever know;
no one knows
except perhaps the old trout
below Joe Lake Dam
and the lake
and the islands
the loon and the sky
that watched and waited;
no one knows.

And in far off Shoreham,
A. Y. Jackson, painting again,
after a "blighty" in France
heard of the upturned canoe
on the lake
and his dreams of camping
and fishing and painting
once more with his friend
came to an end,
as all dreams come
to an end,
as all dreams come
to an end.

Legend has it in Algonquin
Tom Thomson
watches and looks
from the headland
above the bay
on Canoe Lake,
his palette and brushes
and panels in hand
painting the symphony
of the seasons
of his beloved land
he never finished;
the unfolding year,
the folding leaf,
the gathered sheaf,
the winter snow,
the bright bateaux,
painting, painting;
and the great trout
waits in the river
below Joe Lake Dam
and the loon laughs
and sky and lake watch
and only his voice is still
on land and lake
but his spirit is awake
throughout the land he loved
kindling youth to slake
their thirst in beauty.
His spirit is awake,
a torch and a token,
as though a god had spoken;
his spirit is awake,
his spirit is awake.

Arthur S. Bourinot

IF LOVE SHOULD COME

If love should come,
  I wonder if my restless troubled heart,
  Unkind, would bid its visitor depart,
    With chill averted look and pulse unthrilled,
    Because its sanctum was already filled
By cold ambition — would it still be dumb
    If love should come?

If love should come,
  Would all his pleading fall upon my ear
  Unrecked of, as by one who will not hear?
    Would my lips say, "I do not know thy name;
    I seek the far cold heights where dwelleth fame.
In all my life for thee there is no room."
    If love should come?

If love should come,
  Against him would I dare to bar the door,
  And, unregretful, bid him come no more?
    Would stern ambition whisper to my heart,
    "Love is a weakness — bid him hence depart,
For he and I can have no common home,"
    If love should come?

If love should come,
  And I should shut him out and turn away,
  Would what contents me now content me aye?
    Would all success the lonely years might bring
    Suffice to recompense for that one thing?
Ah, *could* my heart be silent, my lips dumb,
    If love should come?

Lucy Maud Montgomery

IN FLANDERS FIELDS

In Flanders fields the poppies blow
Between the crosses, row on row.
  That mark our place; and in the sky
  The larks, still bravely singing, fly
Scarce heard amid the guns below.

We are the Dead. Short days ago
We lived, felt dawn, saw sunset glow,
  Loved and were loved, and now we lie
    In Flanders fields.

Take up our quarrel with the foe:
To you from failing hands we throw
  The torch; be yours to hold it high.
  If ye break faith with us who die
We shall not sleep, though poppies grow
    In Flanders fields.

John McCrae

THE LITTLE BOATS OF BRITAIN
[A Ballad of Dunkirk]

On many a lazy river, in many a sparkling bay,
The little boats of Britain were dancing, fresh and gay;
The little boats of Britain, by busy wharf and town,
A cheerful, battered company, were trading up and down.

A voice of terror through the land ran like a deadly frost:
"King Leopold has left the field, our men are trapped and lost.
No battle-ship can reach the shore, through shallows loud with
    foam;
Then who will go to Dunkirk town, to bring our armies home?"

From bustling wharf and lonely bay, from river-side and coast,
On eager feet came hurrying a strange and motley host,
Young lads and grandsires, rich and poor, they breathed one
    frantic prayer:
"O send us with our little boats to save our armies there!"

Never did such a motley host put out upon the tide:
The jaunty little pleasure-boats in gaudy, painted pride,
The grimy tugs and fishing-smacks, the tarry hulks of trade,
With paddle, oar, and tattered sail, went forth on their Crusade.

And on that horror-haunted coast, through roaring bomb and shell,
Our armies watched around them close the fiery fangs of hell,
Yet backward, backward to Dunkirk they grimly battled on,
And the brave hearts beat higher still, when hope itself was gone.

And there beneath the bursting skies, amid the mad uproar,
The little boats of Britain were waiting by the shore;
While from the heavens, dark with death, a flaming torrent fell,
The little boats undaunted lay beside the wharves of hell.

Day after day, night after night, they hurried to and fro;
The screaming planes were loud above, the snarling seas below.
And haggard men fought hard with sleep, and when their strength
    was gone,
Still the brave spirit held them up, and drove them on and on.

And many a grimy little tramp, and skiff of painted pride
Went down in thunder to a grave beneath the bloody tide,
But from the horror-haunted coast, across the snarling foam,
The little boats of Britain brought our men in safety home.

Full many a noble vessel sails the shining seas of fame,
And bears, to ages yet to be, an unforgotten name:
The ships that won Trafalgar's fight, that broke the Armada's
    pride,—
And the little boats of Britain shall go sailing by their side!

                    Sara E. Carsley

THIS WAS MY BROTHER

This was my brother
At Dieppe,
Quietly a hero
Who gave his life
Like a gift,
Withholding nothing.

His youth...his love...
His enjoyment of being alive...
His future, like a book
With half the pages still uncut—

This was my brother
At Dieppe...
The one who built me a doll house
When I was seven,
Complete to the last small picture frame,
Nothing forgotten.

He was awfully good at fixing things,
At stepping into the breach when he was needed.

That's what he did at Dieppe;
He was needed.
And even death must have been a little ashamed
At his eagerness!

Mona Gould

ALL THERE IS TO KNOW ABOUT
ADOLPH EICHMANN

EYES: .... Medium
HAIR:.. Medium
WEIGHT:.. Medium
HEIGHT: .... Medium
DISTINGUISHING FEATURES:............................ None
NUMBER OF FINGERS:.................................. Ten
NUMBER OF TOES: .... Ten
INTELLIGENCE: .... Medium

What did you expect?
Talons?
Oversize incisors?
Green saliva?

Madness?

Leonard Cohen

THE UNIVERSAL SOLDIER

He's five feet two and he's six feet four.
He fights with missiles and with spears.
He's all of thirty-one and he's only seventeen,
He's been a soldier for a thousand years.

He's a Catholic, a Hindu, an atheist, a Jain,
A Buddhist and a Baptist and a Jew.
And he knows he shouldn't kill and he knows he
always will
Kill for me, my friend, and me for you.
And he's war.

He's the universal soldier and he really is to blame.
His orders come from far away no more.
They come from here-and-there and you-and-me,
and, brothers, can't you see,
This is not the way we put an end to war.

Buffy Sainte-Marie

The Modern

DAYBREAK ON LAKE OPAL: HIGH ROCKIES

as
the
fire
from
opals
a trem
-ulous
dawn be-
gins its
ceremony of
s l o w touch
without palms
its breath with-
out breathing along
the whorled turrets
moving shimmering fall
-ing over the scarred for
-ever-by-the-wind-besieged
ramparts the icecracked tree-
breached walls   the light of
the untouchable Sun sliding from
skyblue into the chill broken flesh
of our lifedrop   warming freeing the
silence of jays and firtops   sending a
heather of wind over unfolding asters and
eaglets   ruffling the moated lake to a green
soul and rolling once more the unpraised sacrifice
of our world into the sword of Its P R E S E N C E

Earle Birney

TREES AT THE ARCTIC CIRCLE
(Salix Cordifolia - Ground Willow)

They are 18 inches long
or even less
crawling under rocks
grovelling among the lichens
bending and curling to escape
making themselves small
finding new ways to hide
Coward trees
I am angry to see them
like this
not proud of what they are
bowing to weather instead
careful of themselves
worried about the sky
afraid of exposing their limbs
like a Victorian married couple

I call to mind great Douglas firs
I see tall maples waving green
and oaks like gods in autumn gold
the whole horizon jungle dark
and I crouched under that continual night
But these
even the dwarf shrubs of Ontario
mock them
Coward trees

And yet — and yet —
their seed pods glow
like delicate grey earrings
their leaves are veined and intricate
like tiny parkas
They have about three months
to ensure the species does not die
and that's how they spend their time
unbothered by any human opinion
just digging in here and now
sending their roots down down down
And you know it occurs to me
                about 2 feet under
those roots must touch permafrost
ice that remains ice forever
and they use it for their nourishment
use death to remain alive

I see that I've been carried away
in my scorn of the dwarf trees
most foolish in my judgements
To take away the dignity
                of any living thing
even tho it cannot understand
                the scornful words
is to make life itself trivial
and yourself the Pontifex Maximus
                of nullity
I have been stupid in a poem
I will not alter the poem
but let the stupidity remain permanent
as the trees are
in a poem
the dwarf trees of Baffin Island

Al Purdy

John Robert Colombo created the following two 'found poems' from pieces of prose which he re-arranged into free-verse form. Here are two from a couple of well-known Canadians.

IMMIGRANTS

Quebec,
April 22nd to 25th,
1831.
One forenoon
I went on board the ship
Airthy Castle,
from Bristol,
immediately after her arrival.
The passengers were in number 254,
all in the hold or steerage;
all English, from about Bristol,
Bath, Frome, Warminster, Maiden Bradley, &c.
I went below,
and truly it was a curious sight.
About 200 human beings,
male and female,
young, old, and middle-aged;
talking, singing, laughing, crying, eating, drinking,
        shaving, washing;
some naked in bed, and others dressing to go
        ashore;
handsome young women (perhaps some)
and ugly old men,
married and single;
religious and irreligious.
Here a grave matron
chaunting selections
from the latest edition
of the last new hymn book;
there, a brawny plough-boy
'pouring forth the sweet melody
of Robin Adair.'
These settlers were poor,
but in general
they were fine-looking people,
and such as I was glad
to see come to America.

They had had a fine passage
of about a month,
and they told me
that no more ship loads of settlers
would come from the same quarter
this year.

I found that it was
the intention of many of them
to come to Upper Canada.
Fortune may smile on some,
and frown on others;
but it is my opinion
that few among them will forget
being cooped up below deck
for four weeks
in a moveable bedroom,
with 250 such fellow-lodgers
as I have endeavoured to describe.

William Lyon MacKenzie

LAST LETTER

Dear General Nieh:

I am fatally ill.
I am going to die.
I have some last favours
to ask of you.

Tell them I have
been happy here,
and my only regret
is that I shall not
be able to do more.

My two cots are for
you and Mrs. Nieh.
My two pairs of English
shoes also go to you.

My riding boots and trousers
I should like to
give to General Lu.

Division Commander Ho
can select what he pleases
from among my things
as a memento from me.

I would like to give
a blanket each to
Shou, my attendant,
and Chang, my cook.

A pair of Japanese shoes
should also go to Shou.

We need 250 pounds of quinine
and 300 pounds of iron compounds
each year. These are for
the malaria and anemia patients.

Never buy medicine
in such cities as
Paoting,
Tientsin and
Peiping again.
The prices there
are twice as much
as in Shanghai
and Hong Kong.

Tell them I have been
very happy. My only regret
is that I shall now
be unable to do more.

The last two years
have been the most significant,
the most meaningful years
of my life. Sometimes it
has been lonely, but I have
found my highest fulfillment
here among my beloved comrades.

I have no strength now
to write more.... To you
and to all my comrades,
a thousand thanks.

                    Norman Bethune

THE LONELY LAND

Cedar and jagged fir
uplift sharp barbs
against the gray
and cloud-piled sky;
and in the bay
blown spume and windrift
and thin, bitter spray
snap
at the whirling sky;
and the pine trees
lean one way.

A wild duck calls
to her mate,
and the ragged
and passionate tones
stagger and fall,
and recover,
and stagger and fall,
on these stones—
are lost
in the lapping of water
on smooth, flat stones.
This is a beauty
of dissonance,
this resonance
of stony strand,
this smoky cry
curled over a black pine
like a broken
and wind-battered branch
when the wind
bends the tops of the pines
and curdles the sky
from the north.

This is the beauty
of strength
broken by strength
and still strong.

A.J.M. Smith

mosaic

oh i can tell you
real canucks
smack of hockey puck
maple syrup
and ex-patriots
dreaming deeper hues
to paint the sunset
or i can be an indian
if i want

tell you how the world
got started
the mountains kept
sliding off
and man snapped
out of his clamshell
telling tiny
wee
white lies

yes i can be an indian
if i want
unearth the bones
of my ancestors
if i have to dynamite
the bloody canadian sheild
(godbless our home and native
landclaim)
to do it

pj johnson

RECLAIMING

The Spirit of Raven is rising
The Wolf howls out to the moon
The day is ripe for honour
As lonely weeps the loon

The land cries out to the people
The people cry out to the land
What price for the soul of the Wolf and Crow
Does anyone understand?
What price for the ancestral homeland
What debt is there need to repay
What ease for the loss of a heritage
That never was given away?

As the stream knows its path to the ocean
The caribou knows where to roam
As each star knows its place in the darkness
A people must know a home
As the crocus knows when to be purple
The salmon knows when it must spawn
So the sleeping bear wakes in the springtime
To reclaim its place in the sun

pj johnson

KOYUKON RIDDLE

Riddle: *Wait, I see something: tiny bits of charcoal*
              scattered in the snow.
Answer: *The bills of ptarmigan.*

> *Julius Jette, Riddles of the Ten' A Indians,*
> *Anthropos, 1913*

She feeds secretly on frozen berries, her soundless passage marked in stitches: white on white embroidery in winter's deceptive light. She conceals her ptarmigan heart in white feathers, her white feathers are concealed in snow. She stills her life in the lifeless snow, but for a bit of charcoal.

The trapper has snowshoed his way uphill for most of the day. He shifts the wages of his living from his shoulder and stoops to adjust the harness when he sees the charcoal in the snow. His eye translates the memory of spectrum-colored flames: the fire that feeds, that dries his clothes, that marks the boundaries of his winter subsistence with warmth and light; the fire that phantoms forth his dreams.

Blue shadows and mauve, snow and feathers drift in his awakening.

C.J. Pettigrew

EVERYTHING IS FREE

Wipe away tears,
Set free your fears:
Everything is free.
Only the lonely
Need much money:
Everything is free.

Don't try to bind
The love you find:
Everyone is free.
Your lover's yours—
Surrender force:
Everyone is free.

The sun melts down,
Spreads gold around:
Everything is free.
The rain is spent
Lending flowers scent:
Everything is free.

The love you live,
The life you give:
Everything is free.

George Elliott Clarke

GRANDFATHER

Grandfather
          Jabez Harry Bowering
strode across the Canadian prairie
hacking down trees
                  and building churches
delivering personal baptist sermons in them
leading Holy holy holy lord god almighty songs in them
red haired man squared off in the pulpit
reading Saul on the road to Damascus at them
Left home
           big walled Bristol town
at age eight
           to make a living
buried his stubby fingers in root snarled earth
for a suit of clothes and seven hundred gruelly meals a year
taking an anabaptist cane across the back every day
for four years till he was whipped out of England

Twelve years old
              and across the ocean alone
to apocalyptic Canada
                Ontario of bone bending child labor
six years on the road to Damascus till his eyes were blinded
with the blast of Christ and he wandered west
to Brandon among wheat kings and heathen Saturday nights
young red haired Bristol boy shoveling coal
in the basement of Brandon college five in the morning

Then built his first wooden church and married
a sick girl who bore two live children and died
leaving several pitiful letters and the Manitoba night

He moved west with another wife and built children and churches
Saskatchewan Alberta British Columbia Holy holy holy
lord god almighty
                    struck his labored bones with pain
and left him a postmaster prodding grandchildren with crutches
another dead wife and a glass bowl of photographs
and holy books unopened save the bible by the bed

Till he died the day before his eighty fifth birthday
in a Catholic hospital of sheets white as his hair

                    George Bowering

THE WOMEN'S JAIL

This garden is outlandish
with its white picket fence
and straggling orchard;
who would guess this painted house
with convent walks
is a women's jail?

Unless you had seen their faces,
old women grey as sponges
drooping in this habitat
young ones sullen
with a worm gnawing them.
I often wonder why the drug-takers
have such skyblue eyes.

And the cheque-forgers:
how velvet they are
how apples and cream,
secretly I envy them
their blossoming bodies
and their talents with men.

Being especially human
I am no judge of evil
but hear how it has
a singing life in them
how it speaks out
with an endowed voice.

Doubt my poor, my gentle one
my overtrained, my fine
my inner ear.

I have been insufficiently dowered
my limbs are pale as winter
sun-starved
my blood is free from alcohol
I am law-abiding, I am completely
resistible—is there anything
praiseworthy in that?

Miriam Waddington

WORDS FROM HELL

(For Brian Ensor, killed in Kingston Penitentiary 18 April 1971)

I was eighteen when I came in these gates
on a sentence of indeterminate duration.
I was eighteen and twisted, and your courts
sent me away from sexual temptation.

I could not keep my fingers off your children.
Your little girls set all my flesh on fire.
I did some things I knew you had forbidden.
You put me in a cell and closed the door.

My need was hideous to the violent men
around me, and they changed my face to mud,
my prisoned life to freedom in the land
of death. Coloured their weapons with my blood.

They beat the life from me with iron bars.
They beat me in a dance of joyous hate.
I cannot count the wounds my body bears.
I was eighteen when I came in these gates.

David Helwig

ON SAINT-URBAIN STREET

My room's bigger than a coffin
but not so well made.
The couple on my left drink, and
at two a.m. the old man shouts
of going back to Russia.
About five he or his wrung-out wife
puke up their passage money.

The janitor (pay, five a week
plus a one-bed apartment
with furnace in kitchen) has
one laughing babe at home
and two girls, for lack of room,
in the orphanage.
On holidays they appear
with their soul-smashed faces.

Upstairs the Negro girl
answers the phone, sings my name
in a voice like a bad angel's.
Her boyfriends change
every weekend, like the movies.
But my room's cheap, tho'
when the wind shifts north
I wear my overcoat
to type this bitter little poem.

Milton Acorn

THE LANDLADY

Through sepia air the boarders come and go,
impersonal as trains. Pass silently
the craving silence swallowing her speech;
click doors like shutters on her camera eye.

Because of her their lives become exact:
their entrances and exits are designed;
phone calls are cryptic. Oh, her ticklish ears
advance and fall back stunned.

Nothing is unprepared. They hold the walls
about them as they weep or laugh. Each face
is dialled to zero publicly. She peers
stippled with curious flesh;

pads on the patient landing like a pulse,
unlocks their keyholes with the wire of sight,
searches their rooms for clues when they are out,
pricks when they come home late.

Wonders when they are quiet, jumps when they move,
dreams that they dope or drink, trembles to know
the traffic of their brains, jaywalks their street
in clumsy shoes.

Yet knows them better than their closest friends:
their cupboards and the secrets of their drawers,
their books, their private mail, their photographs
are theirs and hers.

Knows when they wash, how frequently their clothes
go to the cleaners, what they like to eat,
their curvature of health, but even so
is not content.

And like a lover must know all, all, all.
Prays she may catch them unprepared at last
and palm the dreadful riddle of their skulls—
hoping the worst.

P.K. Page

FOR MUSIA'S GRANDCHILDREN

I write this poem
for your grandchildren
for they will know of your loveliness
only from hearsay,
from yellowing photographs
spread out on table and sofa
for a laugh.

When arrogant
with the lovely grace you gave their flesh
they regard your dear frail body pityingly,
your time-dishonoured cheeks
pallid and sunken
and those hands
that I have kissed a thousand times
mottled by age
and stroking a grey ringlet into place,
I want them suddenly
to see you as I saw you
—beautiful as the first bird at dawn.

Dearest love, tell them
that I, a crazed poet all his days
who made woman
his ceaseless study and delight,
begged but one boon
in this world of mournful beasts
that are almost human:
to live praising your marvellous eyes
mischief could make glisten
like winter pools at night
or appetite put a fine finish on.

Irving Layton

ON MY WAY TO SCHOOL

On my way to school
I used to pass
A Baptist church
And fields of grass.

"Jesus Saves"
Above the gate
Would comfort me
If I were late.

The church is gone,
The street is paved,
The Home Bank thrives
Where Jesus Saved.

Irving Layton

DEATH BY DROWNING

Plunging downward through the slimy water
He discovered, as the fear grew worse,
That life, not death, was what he had been after:
Ironic to die in life's symbol and source.

Drowning was not so easy as it looked from shore.
He had thought of sinking down through layers of peace
To depths where mermaids sang. He would be lapped over
By murmuring waves that lulled him into rest.

But all death is a kind of strangulation,
He had been told once and remembered now,
Choking on water like a rope, and coughing
Its bloody taste from his mouth. He had not known
Before how the body struggled to survive
And must be forced, and forced again, to die.

Elizabeth Brewster

EROSION

It took the sea a thousand years,
A thousand years to trace
The granite features of this cliff,
In crag and scarp and base.

It took the sea an hour one night,
An hour of storm to place
The sculpture of these granite seams
Upon a woman's face.

E.J. Pratt

THE SHARK

He seemed to know the harbour,
So leisurely he swam;
His fin,
Like a piece of sheet-iron,
Three-cornered,
And with knife-edge,
Stirred not a bubble
As it moved
With its base-line on the water.

His body was tubular
And tapered
And smoke-blue,
And as he passed the wharf
He turned,
And snapped at a flat-fish
That was dead and floating.
And I saw the flash of a white throat,
And a double row of white teeth,
And eyes of metallic grey,
Hard and narrow and slit.

Then out of the harbour,
With that three-cornered fin
Shearing without a bubble the water
Lithely,
Leisurely,
He swam—
That strange fish,
Tubular, tapered, smoke-blue,
Part vulture, part wolf,
Part neither—for his blood was cold.

E.J. Pratt

THE STICKHANDLER

Not like the solid defenceman
who, stymied by forecheckers,
can only dump the puck
out to center ice;
or the faithful leftwinger
who diligently patrols his wing
doing what is required of him
& scoring his share of goals…

The phenom steals the puck
in his own zone
& skates around his net
deftly evading his check
fakes a pass
& loops across the blueline
(back & forth goes the puck
at the end of his stick
as if magnetized by willpower,
obedient & sure).
Now he is at center, gathering
speed,
        dodges
the tricky rightwinger
trying to cut him off
stickhandles
round the backward-skating referee
& hair flying, 30 miles per hour,
splits the defence.

Nothing protests.
Even the laws of probability
hold their breath
as the stickhandler makes his final deke
& faking a slapshot
backhands the puck
past the wide-eyed goalie
who stands there frozen,
more like an accomplice
than an opponent.

David Solway

JUMP SHOT

Lithe, quicker than the ball itself;
Spinning through the blocking forearms,
Hands like stars, spread to suspend
The ball from five, and only five,
Magic fingerprints.

The rebound resounding down the pole
And into asphalt, pounded hard by sneakers
Raggedier than the missing-tooth grimaces.
Grimaces. No smiles here. Concentration.
Movement. The calculation.
The arch-back leap. And off the rim again.
Once in ten the satisfying swoosh.

And no time wasted to enjoy it.
Grasp that globe and keep it dribbling:
Elbows were meant for eyesockets;
Work it up higher than hands,
Higher than the grab of gravity.

Working, each man for himself,
Yet deftly, deftly weaving in the pattern.

Richard Peck

THE ANT AND THE ELEPHANT

An elephant of noble stance
And philosophic countenance
Lay smitten, stricken to the core,
Beside his damaged door.

"Alas!" he sobbed, "at last I see
A home is but a mockery.
And therefore I, though big of brain,
Shall never speak again!"

Just then a brisk and friendly ant
Came by to help the elephant.
"What's up?" she asked, and turned to where
His trunk distressed the air.

"You ask me why no hope can cheer
The harmful hurt that haunts me here?—
The doors of yore prevail no more!"
The portly Plato swore.

Indeed, his door was all askew;
The lower hinge would not hang true
Because the bolt had fallen out,
Which splayed the door about.

And now the large philosopher
Unfurled a sort of verbal blur;
"My erstwhile home is occupied—
By homelessness!" he cried.

The kindly insect (who was not
Conversant with the Higher Thought)
Had meanwhile spied the bolt, which lay
An inch or two away,

And with a will she shouldered it,
Although her thorax nearly split.
"...Thus Dwelling dies, and doom descends—
Authentic Language ends!..."

Then up the frame she lugged the thing
With puffs and pants and pummelling,
Until she braced it, half an inch
Above the errant hinge.

"...For what's 'a house' without 'a door?'
The word falls dumb for evermore!
And Truth becomes the nullest nil,
If Language must be still."

Then, while he stroked his intellect,
The insect heaved the door erect,
And somehow managed to cajole
The bolt to fit the hole.

"...For Language is the deepest mode
Of all our being-in-abode;
And thus in silence must I roam—
A mute in my own home!"

But as the metal found its place,
Her feelers caught in the narrow space;
The bolt shot home—and in she went,
A jellied accident.

This roused our hero from his pain
And, since the door was plumb again,
He stepped inside to catch his breath
And explicate her death,

And there, with pachydermic wail,
He voiced the moral of our tale:
One ant, through foolish haste, may fail,
But Truth and Beauty still prevail.

Dennis Lee

WAITER!...
THERE'S AN ALLIGATOR IN MY COFFEE

Waiter!... there's an alligator in my coffee.
Are you trying to be funny?
he said:
what do you want for a dime...?
...a circus?
but sir! I said,
he's swimming
around
and around
in my coffee
and he might—
jump out on the table...
Feed him a lump of sugar! he snarled—
no!...make it two;
it'll weigh him down
and he'll drown.
I dropped two blocks of sugar
into the swamp
two grist jaws snapped them up
and the critter—
he never drowned.
Waiter!...there's an alligator in my coffee.
Kill him! Kill him!
he said:
BASH HIS BRAINS OUT
WITH YOUR SPOON...!
By this time
considerable attention had been drawn:
around my coffee
the waiters, the owner,
and customers gathered.

What seems to be the trouble?
the owner inquired,
and I replied:
There's an alligator in my coffee!
...But the coffee's fresh, he said
and raised the cup up to his nose...
Careful! I said,
he'll bite it
off
and he replied:
How absurd,
and lowered the cup
level to his mouth and
swallowed
the evidence.

Joe Rosenblatt

LIMERICKS

A poet from Winnipeg, Man.,
Wrote verses that never would scan,
    When asked why this was,
    He replied, "Well, because
I always try to fit in as many words to a line as I can."

John Robert Colombo

There once was a time that young men
Could stay with their Atlantic kin,
    But as you may know,
    I'm in high Arctic snow
Wishing I were back home again.

Kevin Michael Kelly

I wish I could fly through the air
With great speed so I could be there
    To stroll through the grasses,
    Or eat golden molasses,
(Or some other fine Maritime fare.)

Elizabeth Courneya

HELLO, MY CHILD

Welcome to the world.
You're new to these parts
I can tell by,
      the clothes you wear,
      and the style of your hair.

We have been waiting for you
not long but wondering ....
      how you are,
      how you will be.

Your room is ready.
Your window has a view
of the future.
What will you see tomorrow?
Which way will your wind blow?

Jeff Boehmer

ON A SCHOOL BOY'S DROWNING

Tonight
nothing has changed:
one ant
sparkles in candlelight,
and others
are making love
in my sugar biscuits.

Life and death
cross like wheat straws
in this strange meadow.

In this land,
we must say
that birds rush after
the chaff of sick sunlight
in burnt-out acres,

Darkness is a tower
whose endless summit
seems to come down
to meet the earth.

Pierre Châtillon

DEATH OF A YOUNG SON BY DROWNING

He, who navigated with success
the dangerous river of his own birth
once more set forth

on a voyage of discovery
into the land I floated on
but could not touch to claim.

His feet slid on the bank,
the currents took him;
he swirled with ice and trees in the swollen water

and plunged into distant regions,
his head a bathysphere;
through his eyes' thin glass bubbles

he looked out, reckless adventurer
on a landscape stranger than Uranus
we have all been to and some remember.

There was an accident; the air locked,
he was hung in the river like a heart.
They retrieved the swamped body,

cairn of my plans and future charts,
with poles and hooks
from among the nudging logs.

It was spring, the sun kept shining, the new grass
leapt to solidity;
my hands glistened with details.

After the long trip I was tired of waves.
My foot hit rock. The dreamed sails
collapsed, ragged.

> I planted him in this country
> like a flag.

Margaret Atwood

SO THIS IS LOVE

So this is love, a kind of sad dance
and who's leading? I lie in bed
without you, your side not slept in
and I don't care. It's over one more time
just like it's raining once again,
a cat dies, you get another. Call it
the same name, remember the generalities,
not the specifics of their small deaths.

It makes me smile how we said this
is different, we've never loved before,
not really *loved*, you know. So here I am
again, trying to work up some kind of anger,
trying to find a word that fits what I
no longer feel.

The cat we got two days ago lies on your pillow,
purrs like he's been there all his life.
Perhaps he has, it's hard to tell the difference.
The rain feels like yesterday's, the long silences,
the same old tired dance.

Lorna Crozier

AFRICVILLE

We are Africville
we are the dispossessed Black of the land
creeping with shadows
with life
with pride
with memories
into the place made for us
creeping with pain away from our home
carrying, always carrying
Africville on our backs
in our hearts
in the face of our child and our anger.

I am Africville
says a woman, child, man at the homestead site.
This park is green; but
Black, so Black with community.
I talk Africville
to you
and to you
until it is both you and me
till it stands and lives again
till you face and see and stand
on its life and its forever
Black past.

No house is Africville.
No road, no tree, no well.
Africville is man/woman/child
in the street and heart Black Halifax,
the Prestons, Toronto.

Wherever we are, Africville,
you and we are that Blackpast homeground.
We mourn for the burial of our houses, our church, our roads;
but we wear Our Africville face and skin and heart.
For all the world.
For Africville.

Maxine Tynes

BONE DANCE

she is not a phenomenon
she is not a magazine story in black and white
with photos before and after

she has just gone home
leaving our faces drawn and thin
it is a clear morning
and she has had a shock
'a shock through my brain'

one day, she said, she ate
a muffin and drank a glass of water

most days she won't say

shopping always for smaller sizes
smaller now than at twelve years
spinning, today, to show us the swirl
a new skirt
she is happy with

for an instant she is lost in color
but stops, white

dizzy, spinning still
she is dizzy more mornings than not
she has always been called dizzy, she says
but she has not always agreed so

she is 82 pounds and counting
down
moving in on her self, hard
as she can be: no excess
no other, no wrong, only

the white of bone, the choreography
of pure form

her dance free of flesh

Lorne Daniel

EVENING IN THE SUBURBS

(after Jacques Prévert)

Around six he arrives
from a hard day at the office
His dog greets him
his children greet him
even his wife greets him
He sits down
his wife sits down
his children sit down
even his dog sits down
and they eat supper
Then he lights his cigar
reads the evening paper
the sports page
the markets
the comics
Gets up
goes into the garden
where he adjusts the sprinkler
turns the water on
sits down again
watching the drops
fall through the air
and goes to sleep
in the deck-chair
When he wakes up
it's dark outside
the sprinkler's off
He lights a cigar
and goes inside
the house is empty
the lights are out
then he remembers
his wife's at the church

his children next door
watching TV
even his dog's gone
He takes a beer
from the refrigerator
but the beer doesn't taste right
he sits down again
in his easy chair
picks up the paper
but his eyes are tired
he doesn't feel like reading
Still he feels like doing something
and he takes the paper
and rips it down the middle
he goes to the kitchen
and takes the beer bottle
and throws it through the window
his dog coming from the cellar
gets booted in the rear
Then he feels better
he feels good again
sits down in his chair
falls asleep like a child.

Raymond Souster

A LECTURE IN ECONOMICS

The airport lunch counter
has a sticky top
The busboy stands with a cloth
listening to the cashier
explain the price of gold
when to buy and when to sell

A man in a mauve turban
is eyeing the hot dog grill
uncertain of the meat
I bought a 90 cent Danish
thinking it was a 70 cent tart
so I'm twenty cents down
The cashier says sell the gold
before a price rise peaks

Walking out I find a dime —
that leaves me ten cents down —
but considering what I've learned
the tuition was quite reasonable

Bert Almon

"I AM TELLING YOU NOW"

I am telling you now
that I have taken my closet—
full of seven shoes, one ice-skate,
too many dresses, three knitting needles,
a jigsaw puzzle with every piece missing,
and a doll that cries real tears—
and stuffed it all into an old, grey sack.
I have let the bugs
out of all the corners
and the cobwebs from out the hats.

I am telling you now
that my closet is empty
of all the little things
I used to have around
to help keep my mind
off the fact that I'm alive.

I am telling you now.

Anne Burnham

LIKE AN ORANGE

When a child
Gives birth
To another child
And when the two

These two lucky children
Look at each other

The earth stops being round
In order to show them
Where to go
And it stretches out
Like an orange skin
    peeled

Jacques Godbout

I, ICARUS

There was a time when I could fly. I swear it.
Perhaps, if I think hard for a moment, I can even tell you the year.
My room was on the ground floor at the rear of the house.
My bed faced a window.
Night after night I lay on my bed and willed myself to fly.
It was hard work, I can tell you.
Sometimes I lay perfectly still for an hour before I felt
        my body rising from the bed.
I rose slowly, slowly until I floated three or four feet
        above the floor.
Then, with a kind of swimming motion, I propelled myself
        toward the window.
Outside, I rose higher and higher, above the pasture fence,
        above the clothesline, above the dark, haunted trees
        beyond the pasture.
And, all the time, I heard the music of flutes.
It seemed the wind made this music.
And sometimes there were voices singing.

Alden Nowlan

ON BEING DETESTED BY A FRIEND

I know of only one person I like
who dislikes me. There could be others.

I like him better
each time I hear
that he's tried again
to injure me;
for he does try,
would turn others
against me if he could;
after the second drink
new acquaintances reveal
he's warned them
I can be savage
—which is true, in a way,
although they don't believe it
or they wouldn't tell me.
I like him better
each time because he does it
so awkwardly, as if
he had never done it
to anyone before
and, afterwards, unless
I'm mistaken, he
despises himself
A good man, obviously.

He and I wave
at each other from our cars,
trade smiles in public places.
This is a small city.
Once or twice a month
we're close enough to talk
and do, very pleasantly.

I don't think he knows yet
that I know he dislikes me
but I'm practically certain
he knows I like him;
he may even be—yes,
I'm almost sure of it,
he may even be
miserable
because of this.

I wonder if there's anyone I don't like
who likes me. I think I would like him.

Alden Nowlan

LOVERS

During the first pogrom they
Met behind the ruins of their homes —
Sweet merchants trading: her love
For a history-full of poems.

And at the hot ovens they
Cunningly managed a brief
Kiss before the soldier came
To knock out her golden teeth.

And in the furnace itself
As the flames flamed higher,
He tried to kiss her burning breasts
As she burned in the fire.

Later he often wondered:
Was their barter completed?
While men around him plundered
And knew he had been cheated.

Leonard Cohen

THE TIME AROUND SCARS

A girl whom I've not spoken to
or shared coffee with for several years
writes of an old scar.
On her wrist it sleeps, smooth and white,
the size of a leech.
I gave it to her
brandishing a new Italian penknife.
Look, I said turning,
and blood spat onto her shirt.

My wife has scars like spread raindrops
on knees and ankles,
she talks of broken greenhouse panes
and yet, apart from imagining red feet,
(a nymph out of Chagall)
I bring little to that scene.
We remember the time around scars,
they freeze irrelevant emotions
and divide us from present friends.
I remember this girl's face,
the widening rise of surprise.

And would she
moving with lover or husband
conceal or flaunt it,
or keep it at her wrist
a mysterious watch.
And this scar I then remember
is medallion of no emotion.

I would meet you now
and I would wish this scar
to have been given with
all the love
that never occurred between us.

Michael Ondaatje

ON MONA'S SMILE

I know what brought
that expression to her face.
During one of her sittings
Leo said to her, "You know, Mona
you're very intelligent
for a woman."

Winona Baker

LIKE TWO SLANT TREES

"Lean on me" he said
loving her weakness
And she leaned hard
adoring his strength
Like two slant trees
they grew together
their roots the wrong way
for standing alone

Fred Cogswell

CABIN FEVER

Most of the time I like you.
Most of the time.
Then there are days
you blink the wrong way
and I want to claw your eyes out.
And you know I love you more
those awful days
when I hold this anger back
and smile
to let you know
it's not you, it's me
and tomorrow
even your backing up
over the cat
won't bother me.

Rodene Zimmer

I AM MAN

I am man
the hunter.

I wound deer
with a car,
squash flies dead
with a swatter,
and eradicate whole species
in just one well-executed oil spill.
Fear me.

I am man
the hunter.

Rodene Zimmer

QUEBEC COUNTRY

here walls are made first to stand
and then to be passed through

to empty: that's my country's word
to empty one's self as well   to empty a lake   to empty
    pockets
to empty a club   to empty a glass   to empty a bottle...
to freeze too... to put hands over one's eyes
to see 8 seasons a year from afar off
4 outside   4 inside
and sometimes if one is real
a couple can be spent inside one's self
here there is no age
and no furniture either
if you scour them too much they are worth less
no my people are ageless
they are neither born nor dead

Claude Péloquin

IN THE YUKON

In Europe, you can't move without going down
      into history
Here, all is a beginning. I saw a salmon jump,
Again and again, against the current,
The timbered hills a background, wooded green
Unpushed through; the salmon jumped, silver.
This was new, was commerce, at the end of the
      summer
The leap for dying. Moose came down to the
      water edge
To drink and the salmon turned silver arcs.
At night, the northern lights played, great over
      country
Without tapestry and coronations, kings crowned
With weights of gold. They were green,
Green hangings and great grandeur, over the north
Going to what no man can hold hard in mind,
The dredge of that gravity, being without
      experience

Ralph Gustafson

RASPBERRY RULES

I pick at five
in the afternoon
greener thumbs drive by
bemused
they pick mornings
finish at eight
fruit frozen by nine

No...
five's the hour
berries ripe and shameless
whole day's heat
caught
between prickly thighs
bees and birds drawn away
to other pleasures
while I have come
to mine

Myrna Garanis

THE DRIVER'S SEAT

My father likes the feel of the wheel
in his hands   foot on the gas
likes to be in control
"You still driving that big Oldsmobile?"
asks a man he meets in the nursing home
my father just there for a visit
not planning to stay

He goes where he wants
when he wants   gives others a lift
has always taken someone else
along for the ride   a car full
of old ladies to church
aunts   cousins and five children
on family holidays

He has a reputation for a heavy foot
got into town in time
to save the life of his hired man
formalin burning away his gut
Now he drives with one foot
on the brake   his tires worn

"You used to ride horses, Dad;
you don't anymore." I try to say
the time has come to turn in the keys
he doesn't always know which one to use
can't find his way home
But he denies his eighty years
two hip replacements
"Bring me a horse," he cries

                    Shirley A. Serviss

THE SMILE

She smiled a smile seen by hundred and thousands of eyes,
Yet it seemed to be only for mine this time.
As she walked closer to me, her eyes sparkled like a pearl
      on the ocean floor.
And her ruby-red lips, wet and inviting
quivered as she drew nearer and nearer ...
And then the smile.
It was almost too much to handle, seeing her after so long,
taking in all of her changes in such a short time, so short,
      too short ...
And then the smile
I held her in my arms, ready to kiss the lips of her beautiful
      face, so beautiful and delicate, drawing nearer and nearer
      until I could feel her breath ...
And then I wake up.
Was it a dream or did this happen?
I wonder?!?
Suddenly there is a shuffling by the door ...
I look,
              And then the Smile!

Joel Sopp

CHANSON

J'ai fait mon ciel d'un nuage
Et ma forêt d'un roseau.
J'ai fait mon plus long voyage
Sur une herbe d'un ruisseau.

D'un peu de ciment: la ville
D'une flaque d'eau: la mer.
D'un caillou, j'ai fait mon île
D'un glaçon, j'ai fait l'hiver.

Et chacun de vos silences
Est un adieu sans retour,
Un moment d'indifférence
Toute une peine d'amour.

C'est ainsi que lorsque j'ose
Offrir à votre beauté
Une rose, en cette rose
Sont tous les jardins d'été.

Gilles Vigneault

SONG

I have made my sky from a cloud
And my forest from a reed.
I have made my longest journey
On a blade of grass in a stream.

From a little plaster, the city;
From a puddle of water, the sea.
From a pebble I made my island
And from an icicle, winter.

Each one of your silences
Is a parting without return
And a moment of indifference
The whole sorrow of love.

Thus it is when I dare
Offer your beauty
A rose, in this rose
Are all the gardens of summer.

Gilles Vigneault
(Translated by A.J.M. Smith)

FUGITIVE

The wind whistled through the pines,
the sky was dark and black,
the wolves howled chillingly at the moon,
and the wind blew steadily at his back.

He plodded on through the snow and blackness,
a fugitive, a castout from society.
The wind cut like a knife
He had killed and now he must flee or die.

The wind had caused the snow to drift
and he strived to make progress.
The snow, his feelings, the memories bogging him down.
He was sinking like a ship in a raging sea.

The will to live was leaving him,
he had no desire to fight or struggle.
He'd taken a life and it haunted him,
He knew he was in trouble.

Trouble now ceased to bother him.
he'd just as soon die as be hunted down like an animal
for they would never forgive him,
his conscience, his memories, would never forgive him.

He laid his weary body in a clump of drifted snow,
and he wandered off to faraway lands.
away from his troubles, his memories, away, just away
In time they would forgive him.

Danny Griffin

can
u
call
it

fr a coupul a
weeks now its bin
bothrin me   on

my mind that
wer robots that
sumwhun   is it god
is programming
us

is god biggr
or smallr than us
six feet is not
very big   if we
cudint see depth
or at leest sum
uv us see depth

what wud happn

we dont live
very long   we weer
out   we relate to
th soshul ideal

eithr for or
against bits uv
improoving heer   polishing ths up theer   smoothr society
if we ar robots   who ar we working for   shud we tell th
othrs   can we get our free will back

bill bissett

THE BALLAD OF OTHELLO CLEMENCE

There's a black wind howlin' by Whylah Falls;
There's a mad rain hammerin' the flowers;
There's a shotgunned man moulderin' in petals;
There's a killer chucklin' to himself;
There's a mother keenin' her posied son;
There's a joker amblin' over his bones.
Go down to the Sixhiboux River, hear it cry,
"Othello Clemence is dead and his murderer's free!"

O sang from Whylah Falls and lived by sweat,
Walked that dark road between desire and regret.
He pitched lumber, crushed rock, calloused his hands:
He wasn't a saint but he was a man.
Scratch Seville shot him and emptied his skull,
Tore a hole in his gut only Death could fill.
Now his martyr-mother witnesses in cries
Over his corpse cankered white by lilies.

There's a black wind snakin' by Whylah Falls;
There's a river of blood in Jarvis Country;
There's a government that don't know how to weep;
There's a mother who can't get no sleep.
Go down to the Sixhiboux, hear it moan
Like a childless mother far, far, from home,
"There's a change that's gonna have to come,
I said, a change that's gonna have to come."

George Elliott Clarke

MODEL PARENTS

There are parents who punish their children.
Others who scold them
Bother them
Badger them
Lecture them
Sicken them
Break them in
Cut them off
Keep them under and
Pull their ears.

Others who reason with them
Jaw them
Worry them
Confine them, bore
Them to death, chide

Them, chivy
Them, crush
Them, curse
Them and disinherit them.

There are also parents who chastise them.
Parents who pinch them
Strike them
Slap them
Spank them
Torment them
Knock them around
Smash them to bits
Hand them over to the Social Welfare and then
Go to bed and make others.

Then there are the ones who
Take away their dessert, keep them
From sleeping, forbid
Them to go out, cut off
Their pockey money, tell them to
Shut up.

Finally, there are those who give them
A good swift kick in the pants and a
Father's blessing on New Year's Day.

Eloi de Grandmont
(Translated from the French by John Glassco)

THE HYPOCRITES AND THE POET

"The people are poor,"
Said the businessman,
"And so we need money
to save them."

"The people are stupid and illiterate,"
said the educator,
"And so we need more money to improve their minds."

"The people are oppressed
and without voice," said the
politician,
"And so we need more money
To elevate them from their plight."

"But the people are warm and beautiful,
And hug me tight in family,"
Said the poet,
"They need only love!"

The businessman received money
And with quick hands constructed
a huge, ridiculous building
with expensive machines
and smiling secretaries —
That produced absolutely nothing,
And a later scandal revealed
He had helped himself generously
To an immense salary, new car
and vacations for his family.

The educator received money
And conducted elaborate research
on the "Whyfores" of this
and the "Wherefores" of that,
That proved little more than
what was already known,
And he was showered with praise,
And his edition bound in gold,
Only then to be committed to shelves
to collect dust,
While the people remained puzzled and astray
In institutions that ruined them.

The politician received money,
And quickly gobbled it up
on gambling debts,
Though careful manner and
timely speeches,
Enabled him to maintain his stature
among the poor,
Though a few more aware
Challenged his name in public,
And caused him in private moments
to say:
"Look at these goddamned people,
They're not worth a goddamned thing."

The poet received none —
But the fierce honesty
of his words,
Opened doors inside the
people's minds,
And they flocked to see him
and listened intently to his words,
And with new inspiration —
They constructed buildings, wrote new books.
And the people and the poet
Learned from each other and grew immensely,
And they did it with love,
And only love.

David Woods

NATIVE SONG

(For Cyril & Rosella Fraser)

We find ourselves in purpose steeped,
To wrestle pain from these tired hands,
And erect new hope in the dark
horizon,
Beyond the reach of those who command.

A racist man's tools —
His education, his erudite words,
Have kept us closed,
We are not relieved by ecstatic
devotion to God,
Or by easy wish,
Despite all involvements
An agonized cry still emits from the soul.

Old men and old women
Know of the horror of those days,
When young and dressed in Sunday-fine,
They made their way to town,
And were fixed contemptuously
by white eyes —
Hounded from dust till dawn
Till their hopes were crushed,
And their sense of freedom died.

And drunk remembrances of old men
Of old days and old glories,
Or Mom Suse, Pearleen Oliver
that type,
Whose love rose like a sun
through the miasmal haze.

Yet as we wander in bowed status,
In minds estranged from themselves,
Dance as we always dance
In the old hall, or late-night club
What song shall rise from the
throat?
What great task will seize the hands?

And if that Preston man in inspired
vision
had not set about to construct
his itinerant church,
Or Mrs. Best — awakened by study —
Had not asserted her womanly pride,
Or that Jones man had not considered and
meant his violence,
What would we be then?
Cadavers arranged like logs
Moving along a stink river
Not ours
But flowing on — lost forever.

An acrid mist rises above the land,
The sad breath of mother earth,
Tired of having weaned children
in deep cradles of human love:
Lucasville, Sunnyville, North Preston,
Weymouth Falls,
Children who are abandoned
And are left sad without choice.

I will go on my way
With a clear conviction,
To break these Nova Scotian
chains
So that a girl can decide
in a real way
To seize the earth by storm,
Or to sit back quietly into
the bosom of earth,
Nurtured by a long and ancient
love.
And I will fight — as wickedly
as the devil fights,
All that stifles her breath.

And when the sun settles
like a tired eyelid —
On the failed promise of Preston,
And ghosts of old appear,
I will sing a song
And that song will be beautiful,
And that song will be great,
And no man on earth will be able
to block it from his ears.
And this will be my monument
Collected from the beauty and
pain,
Of all those who have lived
and died
In the hungry chambers
of the black dream.

David Woods

CROSSING TO BRENTWOOD
ON THE MILL BAY FERRY
—*November 4, 1975*

Now, for the moment, everything is promised.
It is a calm bright day.
Not even any mist over the trees,
nor ice in the slippery roots.
No sense of urgency.

We are crossing the water.
I hold your hand needing
only that. The bare sea is simple enough
and the clean sky that no longer seems
lonely. Birds circle the boat
full of their good messages.

Last night snow fell on the
mountains. I woke up
shivering and afraid.
I needed to know everything about you.
Suddenly I needed to know
more than what there was.

Today, for the moment, everything is forgotten.
I hold your warm hand as if it were something
I had just found wanting to be held and
you smile back. Later when we talk
ours will be other voices.
Now, crossing the water,
I am certain there is only us.

Susan Musgrave

HOUDINI

I suspect he knew that trunks are metaphors,
could distinguish between the finest rhythms
unrolled on rope or singing in a chain
and knew the metrics of the deepest pools

I think of him listening to the words
spoken by manacles, cells, handcuffs,
chests, hampers, roll-top desks, vaults,
especially the deep words spoken by coffins

escape, escape: quaint Harry in his suit
his chains, his desk, attached to all attachments
how he'd sweat in that precise struggle
with those binding words, wrapped around him
like that mannered style, his formal suit

and spoken when? by whom? What thing first said
'there's no way out?'; so that he'd free himself,
leap, squirm, no matter how, to chain himself again,
once more jump out of the deep alive
with all his chains singing around his feet
like the bound crowds who sigh, who sigh.

Eli Mandel

LAZY GREY MORNING

cafe au lait
and fruit
on a rain darkened
balcony

the porter
braided and moustached
a fat grandee
raving discretely
against Madrid
extolling his brother
who went to America
when he was twelve
and is now rich
in New York

he serves *El Diario*
the mail   coffee
and   small gossip
which we drink
eagerly

his hand   cobra
quick
palms his tip
this small difficulty
surmounted
he bows himself out
while we watch
admiring   waylaid but
smiling

Claire Harris

EENIE MEENIE MYNEE MOE

Contingency and gene mutation
Genetic drift and isolation,
All of this and repetition
Led to life in this rendition.
In every locus, niche or place
Adaptation is a race.
Survivors so become the winners
Losers often simply dinners.
Flight not fight and surreption
Win for some the competition.
Some achieved the high distinction
Of special sudden mass extinction,
Becoming mere apostrophes
By losing to catastrophes
And dissappearing into voids
Erased by cosmic asteroids.
All in part are some solution
To the fact of evolution.
Circumstance enhanced by chance
Is real in every nook you glance.
The force that acts in this direction
Is luck and natural selection.

Luigi Pietro Visentin

STELLA FUNERALIA

Blinks and winks celestial
Are semaphores of night,
That make a fool observer
Feel mortal at the sight.
Angst is but a feeling
In those who contemplate
A space-time life exclusive
Questioning their fate.
Cosmic rays and microwaves,
The red-shift lights you see
Are astronomic elegies
That signal in the sky
A very common ending for
They live and then they die

Luigi Pietro Visentin

THE YELLOW SILK DRESS

magnolia yellow, butter
yellow of yellow roses,
sun whipped in cream
of white heifer, god-conjured,
gleaming warmer than gold, than sun,
a vinery, stitchings, thread tracings,
petals embroidered
and silk-covered buttons,
a demure line of dots,
elliptical,
gliding, *glissando*, towards
silk-scalloped waist,
slight flare of skirt
rippling to mid-calf hem

a rhapsody of curves and of silk
breathing out mothballs, faintly,
'forties romance—
essence of tangos—of twos—
hanging in the thrift store,
flirty, on the hook,
cooing, "uncrumple me—iron me,
wear me tonight,
step out in my curves,
my soft yellow silk—
i can hear the rustle
somewhere in the city
of a lean tuxedo
a dress shirt all ruffles
and golden snake cufflinks,
an emerald stud—
stars and champagne"

Mary Dalton

TAXI DISPATCHER JAZZ

where you at, five five
where you headed at
pickin up a job are yah

car forty-five
Holiday Holiday
gotta go to main door—
justholdonforaminutewillyah

three six four
there by Shoppers'—
Used Cars—
there by City Motors

don't call me Harry, Darren
Roger's not my name either

St. John's staccato
barking the pockets of the city
a twitch of demented riffs
these cats under hot tar roofs
an irritable music
authentic as fiddle
        as washboard
as any
        cigarette papers and comb

Mary Dalton

UP-ALONG

An aching wanderlust
that wouldn't be denied
caused him to quit
his rock.
Leaving the dust
he was moving
up-along
where even the narrowest lane
was under tar.

Toronto
had three syllables
for him then
with accent
on the middle one.
"Go'in up-along,"
he'd proudly told his friends.
"A fancy car
a mainland piece of stock
and buildings higher even
than Sir Richard Squires
in Corner Brook."

He was limping up
from Newfoundland
in a hundred ninety-seven dollar pile
of chrome and steel;
odometer unhooked
four years ago.
Must be a hundred thousand
on her now
at least.
Balloon-smooth tires
crooning a siren lay
rushing a rock-born pilgrim
through the night
toward
the New Jerusalem.

Some relatives
up there
had promised him
there'd be no problem
hooking up a job;
his brother-in-law
had started out
at three-fifteen an hour
a year ago.
"Come up," they said.
"We'll help you
find a job."

Within a week
those gifted hands
that had created model ships
worked on a line
that mass-produced
soft, antiseptic
toilet rolls;
material
that guaranteed
it would not irritate
the haemorrhoids
of Bay Street dowagers.

The letters home
flamboyantly
described the visits
to city hall
the Gardens and
he'd seen so many people
wearing flowers
in their hair.

His mother
did not read
between the lines...

On New Year's Day
it was reported
on the front page
of "The Globe and Mail"
that Princess Anne
expressed imperious impatience
with the press
for showing some concern
about a mild abrasion
on her hand.

Some twenty pages farther
in "The Globe"
there was brief mention
that last night
some man had
killed himself
in falling
thirty storeys down.
It failed to say
the building had been taller even
than Sir Richard Squires
in Corner Brook.

Wasn't it strange
that when a man
could finally say
Toronto
with two syllables
he'd do a thing like that?

Enos D. Watts

PRECISION

As a geological proposition
the island
could have never been there;
but from all compass points
it withstood the assault
of ignorant waves
that struck out blindly
taking only
the weakest part of the rock.

And men would mark
new margins
for the sea.

Yet other horn-rimmed
vertically moving
young men,
though unschooled
in the barter of tears,
drew neat symmetrical paradigms
and did
on some leisurely afternoons
more than the sea could do
in a thousand years.

Enos D. Watts

PEPPERMINT ROCK

If somebody asked me
for my earliest memory,
it would have to be
that day in Avalon
when I, just a drooling toddler,
dropped a great peppermint knob
into my infant brother's mouth.
There in the crib cage,
below a framed picture
of somebody's guardian angel,
he was kicking and crying,
a gaping hole of a mouth,
one chasm of grief
through which my world
was tumbling.
To appease the spirit
of this pit,
I rolled one of my precious
candy boulders
to the brink of the lip
and let it slip...

Here everything goes mad:
the baby, blue-black
swirls upside down
and mother
is slapping his back.
She is shouting at me.
I scurry under a table,
her wrath like a dogfish
after me.

I wait for that worst
which always happens.
Up in the glassy pictures
the ancestors all frown down.
Queen Victoria grows
another layer on her chin.
The guardian angel goes
for his or her sword...
The candy,
a slimy shiny ball,
chuckles on the floor...

I can laugh at it now,
the way I tried
to stuff his face that day.
It is only in my moralizing
moments
or bouts of self-pity
that I want to change this poem
and call it my earliest lesson:
how a gesture of pure
unadulterated generosity
can be so misunderstood,
or an act of kindness
can sometimes kill.

Tom Dawe

GRANNY GLOVER'S DREAM

(from a picture of the same name by David Blackwood)

A long thin line
thinner and thinner as it goes
becomes a dot
disappears where there is nothing

these are the villagers
they are leaving their village
huddled into the wind
they are going away

out where there is nothing
they have gone away to nothing
the long thin line dissolves itself
into the emptiness of snow

at the end of the line
turned to the wind
she stands looking back

if she had been farther up the line
she could have been spared this instant
but where she is
at the end of it
she is forced to confront
face to face
the final moment of their going

in a second
when this scene unfreezes itself
she will turn
become again the last of the line
will turn and walk away
will become nothing in the windy distance

in this instant however
she is frozen where she is
solidified against the wind
turned back toward the house

on the window a flower pot
and in it a flower bloomed open
to the day's bright light
outside everything is frozen still
everything except the wind

and the wind's white howling

Al Pittman

AT A WOOLCO STORE RECENTLY

At a Woolco store recently
I was surprised (to say the least)
by the sudden sight of workers
heading all in one direction
through the aisles
Young clerks from men and boys wear
girls from lingerie
old ladies from cosmetics
all met, locked arms together firmly
under strong fluorescent lights
beaming star-like, saying nothing
Till far out from behind them
music struck aloud
and joining in precisely
they broke out proud in song
like a thousand rebel members
of some tabernacle choir!
Bright red with anger, white with rage
their robust notes rang strong
"Ohhh Cannn - a - daa
Glorrr - i - uss and freee…!"
And on and on
singing masterly to a crescendo
I was enthralled, infatuated, swollen-hearted
I threw away my purchases in answer to their call!
They held me there dumbfounded
Tears of patriotism from my eyes began to fall……

But as I ran to join them
I was cut surely to a stop
For over the loud speaker, louder than them all
came the voice of the store manager
breaking out in southern drawl
"Personnel from musical equipment
to checkout number three"
and cut their rhythm, balance, poise
like a beaver's tail gone mad
......Blue with fury, but biting hard
they turned away dry-lipped, defeated
to their departments once again
And I, I turned aside lackluster
bent, took my articles
and walked meekly through the store.

Kevin Major

BLOOD AND WATER

I often wondered what it would be like
To have a step-child,
And now I think I know;
I got her by marriage
Though not in the usual way,
this child of mine
Is almost eighty now,
And I am forty-eight.

"Blood is thicker than water,"
My mother used to tell me,
And I hated for her to say it.
I didn't know what it meant
For one thing,
And it sounded ugly.

But now, unnerved, I'm beginning
To wonder
If it's true,
How else can I explain
The way I feel
Toward this patient creature
Who never harmed anyone
In her life,
Especially me?

She was given to me,
I didn't ask for her,
And her daily presence
Makes me want to run,
Friends marvel at how well
I treat her
As if they were talking about
A farmer
With a worn-out work-horse.

And so we stay together
This meek-faced, uncomplaining step-child
And me,
And what I feel for her
Is a mixture
Of pity, irritation, and more pity,
But never love.

As I serve her meals and wash
Her shameful laundry,
And try to talk to her
(The hardest thing of all),
I realize with terror
That she loves me,
Why doesn't blood and water
Work for her?

Helen Porter

I HEAR YOU'RE LOOKING

I hear you're looking
for your soul
somewhere in the mountains
near Katmandu
I wish you luck
however
I think your search
is futile
as the place
is full of souls
and you'll never know
which one is yours

Des Walsh

ON POETRY, LOVE, & DEATH

Poetry, like love,
like death,
is something
I know nothing
about

other than
all three

should be
approached
with the utmost
caution.

Des Walsh

THE MURDERER

My uncle's best friend
Went mad
And killed his wife
And their two children.
They locked him up,
On the advice of the court psychiatrist,
In a small room with no windows.
There are bars on the door.

My cousin,
Who is quite a daring young woman,
Went to visit him.
He told her that
He thought he had killed his wife,
But he couldn't remember why.
He was sure he shouldn't have done it.
He didn't mention the children.

When I first heard of him,
I felt very sorry for his wife,
And their two young children.
Now I feel sorry for my uncle's best friend,
Who must sit in that little room
With no windows,
All alone with a murderer.

Wanda Legge

This poem was inspired by a true event. Legge had read of a man who had committed murders when he was insane, and who some years later had begun to recover his sanity. The ultimate environment, the poet seems to suggest, is the self.

UMBRELLA POEM

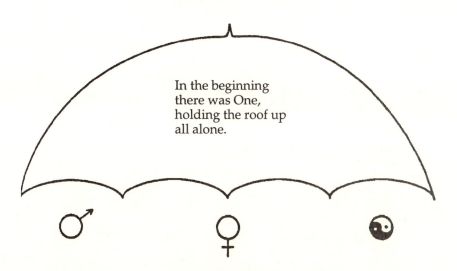

In the beginning
there was One,
holding the roof up
all alone.

One was clever,
invented Two—
nice—accepting—
joy! calloo!
—found at length it
wouldn't do—
or, more likely,
always knew
time would wear the
plaything through.

One was clumsy:
darling Two
got mislaid or
slipped from view:
haunted forest,
space, ensue.

One was lucky:
God sent Two,
with a note its
name was *You*—
magic word to
make things new!
out of One, be-
hold, *I* grew.

Rooftree—wordtree—
space—time—friend—
make some shelter,
till the end.

Jay Macpherson

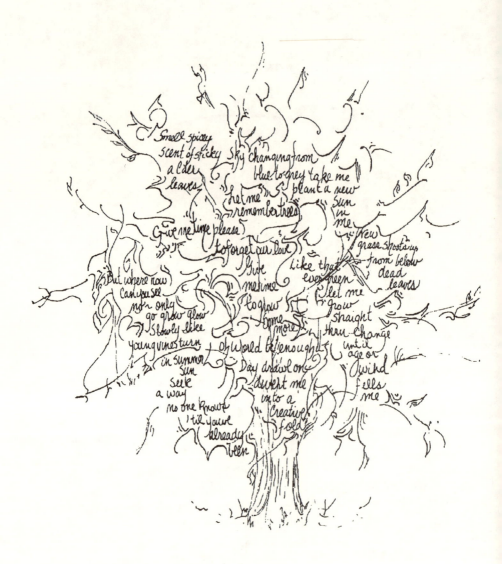

Judy Copithorne

HAIKU (1)

dawn flecks
in lees
of buttercup

doryman
lifts herring-net
and morning moon

Tom Dawe

HAIKU

Night is a nun; her
cloth-coffined back is shadow
to her white-faced sun.

John Robert Colombo

HAIKU (5)

lying in alders
waiting for loon's cry
to take shape

water strider
stirring clockwise
on the moon

Tom Dawe

HAIKU

beyond the school door
a butterfly free of bells
slides on wind

Claire Harris

Into the 21st Century

New Immigrant Voices

CHINESE CAMP, KAMLOOPS
(circa 1883)

in the photograph he stands alone
under a willow
before the small tent
the shadows are long
likely an evening in early july
his left foot is extended slightly
beyond the other
on the edge of his shadow
at the base of the tree
two washbasins lean perfectly
against one another
like two coins in a child's hand
his clothes are baggy
his arms are flexed
you would like to be romantic
and believe he is reading
a letter from his parents back home
or a letter from some young lady
he possibly dreaming of her small delicate hands
tiny feet
and body smooth and soft as silk
exactly the way it was supposed to be
if your family were rich
and you were a girl
growing skilful at some craft
you constantly sitting
to ease the pain from tiedup feet
knowing the suitors and matchmakers
would always ask
'let see feet...how small?'
the oriental myth
the smaller the feet
the softer the body
but no...if this young man had a sweetheart
she was likely poor
and walked to work
like the rest of the family
simply surviving
her feet growing naturally...

looking closer at the photograph
you become realistic
and realize...no
there are no letters for this lonely man
he is only rolling
a cigarette

2
in the second photograph
his two friends
standing ten feet apart
actually pose:
one smiling
and revealing
a missing tooth
...the other
an unusually tall man
looking
almost stately
a stern face
that might have been
the face of an emperor
behind them
a simple table
and two stools
in the shade
of a tree

3
by the third photograph
oriental clothes have been worn out
it's likely another summer
the men are wearing cowboy hats
and pointed riding boots
the new clothes fit more snugly
across angular bodies seeming thinner
and solid
as anvils

Andrew Suknaski

WHAT DO I REMEMBER OF THE EVACUATION?

What do I remember of the evacuation?
I remember my father telling Tim and me
About the mountains and the train
And the excitement of going on a trip.
What do I remember of the evacuation?
I remember my mother weeping
A blanket around me and my
Pretending to fall asleep so she would be happy
Though I was so excited I couldn't sleep
(I hear there were people herded
Into the Hastings Park like cattle.
Families were made to move in two hours
Abandoning everything, leaving pets
And possessions at gun point.
I hear families were broken up
Men were forced to work. I heard
It whispered late at night
That there was suffering) and
I missed my dolls.
What do I remember of the evacuation?
I remember Miss Foster and Miss Tucker
Who still live in Vancouver
And who did what they could
And loved the children and who gave me
A puzzle to play with on the train.
And I remember the mountains and I was
Six years old and I swear I saw a giant
Gulliver of Gulliver's Travels scanning the horizon
And when I told my mother she believed it too
And I remember how careful my parents were
Not to bruise us with bitterness
And I remember the puzzle of Lorraine Life
Who said "Don't insult me" when I
Proudly wrote my name in Japanese
And Tim flew the Union Jack
When the war was over but Lorraine
And her friends spat on us anyway
And I prayed to God who loves
All the children in his sight
That I might be white.

Joy Kogawa

I FIGHT BACK

ITT ALCAN KAISER
Canadian Imperial Bank of Commerce
These are privileged names in my Country
But I AM ILLEGAL HERE

My Children Scream
My Grandmother is dying

I came to Canada
And Found the Doors
Of Opportunities Well Guarded

I Scrub Floors
Serve Backra's Meals on Time
Spend two days working in one
And Twelve Days a Week

Here I Am in Canada
Bringing Up Someone Else's Child
While someone Else and Me in Absentee
Bring Up My Own

AND I FIGHT BACK

And Constantly they ask,
"Oh Beautiful Tropical Beach
With Coconut Tree and Rum,
Why did you Leave There
Why on Earth did you Come?"

AND I SAY:
  For the Same Reasons
  Your Mothers Came

I FIGHT BACK

They label me
Immigrant, Law-breaker, illegal
Ah No, Not Mother, Not Worker, Not Fighter

I FIGHT BACK
Like my Sisters Before Me
I FIGHT BACK
I FIGHT BACK

Lillian Allen

INSPECTION OF A HOUSE PAID IN FULL

I could not hide
my curiosity at your pride
in paying cash in full

perhaps it was
because you arrived
in canada
young and penniless

while working at our restaurant
you came up with the strangest notion
that some day
when you own your own place
you could get away
with substituting ink
for coffee

(cheap profitable imitation)

those wild hopeful impossibilities
made yours a rocky one man road
up the golden mountain

yet you made it

and today
looking me squarely in the eye
you tell me you have arrived
your family at your side

my last words
are

BEWARE THE TAXMAN

Jim Wong-Chu

POEM FOR MY DAUGHTER

Toys, the blue rhinoceros with the spidery lashes,
the monkey coyly seeing no evil,
hands taped over his eyes,
a truth barrier, his long sad tail
like a phallus soft with spent love,
the flower rattle, the pink squeeze-toy
and an Indian doll whose black braid you use
to tug her along,
such are the objects you have so far
to know yourself.

Emily, these baubles that people your world
have no desires of their own,
baby woman, what can I tell you to try to be
without being wrong?

Try to live intelligently and be happy
as you are
as your mother read too many books
thinking she could not be pretty.

A single season may strike campfires in a man's blood.
Keep what you feel underground.
Only the lead in your pencil
as you note these things
need poison your reflection
wanting the power that can make an old bone
rise.
Few men may come back from the dead for you.

I can tell you this because I have found a man's duty
a cold bed to sleep in
and his lust a fast train,
because you are not unique,
you who have so soon discovered your hands and feet,
because even Sartre betrayed Simone de Beauvoir
for every half-baked dish in Paris,
I advise you to steel yourself
although there's no escape from pain
you can burnish with it
like an iron in the fire.

Mary di Michele

ON A RACIST TERRAIN

Facing blocks
Struggling to walk
On a racist terrain
On a sexist terrain.

Aching with pain
           of disdain
Is my only gain
On this terrain.

Groping in the dark
Path unknown
I lost what was my own
My name and the sense of who I am.

Bewildered and alone
I struggle on my own
Facing blocks
On the racist terrain
On the sexist terrain.

Feeling defeat
Yearning to retreat
To the home I owned
And the comfort of knowing my name
and what I owned.

Yearning in heart
Is a thought
Which is locked
Under a rock
And the blocks
On the racist terrain.

I ache but can't scream
Because I lost
The voice I owned
In my home
On the racist terrain
On the sexist terrain.

I forgot who I am.

                    Nayyar Javed

A Selection of
Poet-Songwriters

NORTHWEST PASSAGE

Ah, for just one time, I would take the Nortwest Passage
To find the hand of Franklin reaching for the Beaufort Sea
Tracing one warm line through a land so wide and savage
And make a Northwest Passage to the sea

Westward from the Davis Strait, 'tis there 'twas said to lie
The sea-route to the Orient for which so many died
Seeking gold and glory, leaving weathered broken bones
And a long-forgotten lonely cairn of stones

Three centuries thereafter, I take passage overland
In the footsteps of brave Kelso, where his "sea of flowers" began
Watching cities rise before me, then behind me sink again
This tardiest explorer, driving hard across the plain

And through the night, behind the wheel, the mileage clicking West
I think upon Mackenzie, David Thompson and the rest
Who cracked the mountain ramparts, and did show a path for me
To race the roaring Fraser to the sea

How then am I so different from the first men through this way?
Like them I left a settled life, I threw it all away
To seek a Northwest Passage at the call of many men
To find there but the road back home again

Stan Rogers

THE MARY ELLEN CARTER

She went down last October in a pouring driving rain,
The skipper, he'd been drinking, and the mate, he felt no pain.
Too close to Three Mile Rock and she was dealt her mortal
    blow
And the Mary Ellen Carter settled low.
There was just us five aboard her when she finally was awash.
We'd worked like hell to save her, all heedless of the cost
And the groan she gave as she went down, it caused us to
    proclaim
That the Mary Ellen Carter would rise again.

Well, the owners wrote her off; not a nickel would they spend.
"She gave twenty years of service, boys, then met her sorry
    end.
"But insurance paid the loss to us, so let her rest below",
Then they laughed at us and said we had to go.
But we talked of her all winter, some days around the clock,
For she's worth a quarter million, afloat and at the dock.
And with every jar that hit the bar we swore we would remain
And make the Mary Ellen Carter rise again.

CHORUS
Rise again, rise again, that her name not be lost
To the knowledge of men.
All those who loved her best and were with her til the end
Will make the Mary Ellen Carter rise again.

All spring, now, we've been with her on a barge lent by a
    friend.
Three dives a day in a hard hat suit and twice I've had the
    bends—
Thank God it's only sixty feet and the currents here are slow
Or I'd never have the strength to go below.
But we've patched her rents, stopped her vents, dogged hatch
    and porthole down,
Put cables to her, 'fore and aft and girded her around.
Tomorrow, noon, we hit the air and then take up the strain
And watch the Mary Ellen Carter rise again.

CHORUS

For we couldn't leave her there, you see, to crumble into
  scale—
She'd saved our lives so many times, living through the gale
And the laughing, drunken rats who left her to a sorry grave
They won't be laughing in another day....
And you, to whom adversity has dealt the final blow
With smiling bastards lying to you everywhere you go,
Turn to, and put out all your strength of arm and heart and
  brain
And, like the Mary Ellen Carter rise again!

Rise again, rise again—though your heart be broken
And life about to end.
No matter what you've lost, be it a home, a love, a friend—
Like the Mary Ellen Carter, rise again.

                    Stan Rogers

BROKEN ARROW

Who else is gonna bring you
   A broken arrow
Who else is gonna bring you
   A bottle of rain
There he goes, moving across the water
There he goes turning my whole
   world around

Do you feel what I feel
Can we make that so it's part of the deal
I gotta hold you in these arms of steel
Lay your heart on the line...this time

I wanna breathe when you breathe
When you whisper like that hot
   summer breeze
Count the beads of sweat that cover me
Didn't you show me a sign, this time

Who else is gonna bring you
   A broken arrow
Who else is gonna bring you
   A bottle of rain
There he goes, moving across the water
There he goes turning my whole
   world around

Can you see what I see
Can you cut behind the mystery
I will meet you by the witness tree
Leave the whole world behind

I want to come when you call
I'll get to you if I have to crawl
They can't hold me with these iron walls
We've got mountains to climb

Who else is gonna bring you
  A broken arrow
Who else is gonna bring you
  A bottle of rain
There he goes, moving across the water
There he goes turning my whole
  world around

Robbie Robertson

SOUTHERN BOYS

Southern Boys are warm and lovely
They speak gently of their homes
And show you pictures
of the folks
Their breath in your ear
is as soft as the cotton
Whether they're wooing
or whispering
The latest racist joke

CHORUS
I get knocked right off my feet
When I hear that Southern drawl
And I don't mind the pain
'Cause the feeling's worth the fall

Buttered grits is fare
for breakfast
And if you like and your
aim is good
Maybe a squirrel
Then around nine we tap
that moonshine

And it's on out to the porch
for a moonlight swing
With me, your Northern girl

CHORUS
I got knocked right off my feet
When I hear that Southern drawl
And I don't mind the pain
'Cause the feeling's worth the fall

Were you born?
Where do you come from?
Is your tropic in Cancer?
Is your sun sign divine?
Let it out oh please don't hide it
All that good ol' stuff
Down below that
Mason-Dixon line

CHORUS
I get knocked right off my feet
When I hear that Southern drawl
And I don't mind the hurt
'Cause the feeling's worth the fall
And I don't extend your hand
'Cause I couldn't move at all

Kate McGarrigle

SALLY'S SONG

(to "Wee Geordie" for being part of my circle - R)

On the top of Sally's house is a weather vane,
It's come undone and points out to the sky.
Right beside the Bay of Fundy's shores of rusty red,
That's where Sally lived and where she died.

I think about you Sally now I'm living in your house,
I look out of your windows on the sea,
Where you watched the seasons come and go and take
        your years away,
Until you died when you were eighty-three.

CHORUS
And Sally, O, Sally, you were quite a gal
They say you went to war in forty-two,
And kept a canteen for the troops
And worked right at the front
An independent woman, that was you.

I often think about you when I walk along the shore
To look for treasures washed in on the tide
Pebbles softened by the years and feathers from the gulls
Moonshells that are worn to smooth inside.

Up in the attic, a bundle of letters,
A photo of you with a tall handsome soldier,
Leaning against an old rock wall somewhere in Europe,
You look so devil-may-care and so beautiful.

CHORUS

I want to tell you Sally, there's a baby in your house,
His hair is silky black—his eyes are blue
I think of how life circles round, and ends begin again
Sometimes I look at him and think of you.

And Sally—your daffodils just opened up today,
The fog is lifting and the sun is starting to burn through,
I wish that I had known you
And I feel sometimes I do
An independent woman, that was you.

CHORUS

I wish that I had known you
And I feel sometimes I do
An independent woman, that was you.
An independent woman, that was you.

On the top of Sally's house is a weather vane...

Rose Vaughan

SOAP BOX PREACHER

Soap box preacher standing on the corner
And all the people they would gather round
You speak of faith with a blaze of glory
But those that fear they wanna knock you down

Nobody knows where you live
Where do you go in the naked night
All of the prophets that come before you
They can hear your lonesome cry

When you're out there in the night
All alone
When you're staring in the light
At the end of the road

CHORUS:
In those proud shoes, coming on up the alley
In those proud shoes, walks all over the sky
Then he tipped his hat just like Don Quixote
And said don't let the rapture pass you by

Heard a bugle blowing in the misty morning
What a haunting sound over Times Square
Heard of the ghost of 52nd Street
Looked out the door but no one was there

Out in the cold Harlem rain
I went looking for this minstrel man
Played me a song to ease the pain
With a salvation army band

When you're out there in the dark
All alone
When you're sleeping in the park
At the end of the road

CHORUS

In the neon wilderness and the asphalt jungle
He carries his cross of passion
Through the wreckage and the rumble

CHORUS:
In those proud shoes, coming on up the alley
In those proud shoes, walks all over the sky
Then he tipped his hat just like Don Quixote
And said don't let the rapture
Don't let the rapture pass you by

Don't let it pass you by

Robbie Robertson

DON QUIXOTE

Through the woodland, through the valley
Comes a horseman wild and free.
Tilting at the windmills passing,
Who can the brave young horseman be?

He is wild but he is mellow.
He is strong but he is weak.
He is cruel but he is gentle.
He is wise but he is weak.

Reaching for his saddlebag,
He takes a battered book into his hand.
Standing like a prophet bold,
He shouts across the ocean to the shore
'Til he can shout no more.

"I have come o'er moor and mountain
Like the hawk upon the wing.
I was once a shining knight
Who was the guardian of a king.

I have searched the whole and over
Looking for a place to sleep.
I have seen the strong survive
And I have seen the lean grow weak.

See the children of the earth
Who wake to find the table bare.
See the gentry in the country
Riding off to take the air."

Reaching for his saddlebag,
He takes a rusty sword into his hand.
Then striking up a knightly pose,
He shouts across the ocean to the shore
'Til he can shout no more.

"See the jailer with his key
Who locks away all trace of sin.
See the judge upon the bench
Who tries the case as best he can.

See the wise and wicked ones
Who feed upon life's sacred fire.
See the soldier with his gun
Who must be dead to be admired.

See the man who tips the needle.
See the man who buys and sells.
See the man who puts the collar
On the ones who dare not tell.

See the drunkard in the tavern,
Stemming gold to make ends meet.
See the youth in ghetto black,
Condemned to life upon the street."

Reaching for his saddlebag,
He takes a tarnished cross into his hand.
Standing like a preacher now,
He shouts across the ocean to the shore.

Then in a blaze of tangled hooves,
He gallops off across the dusty plain
In vain to search again
Where no one will hear.

Through the woodland, through the valley
Comes a horseman wild and free.
Tilting at the windmills passing,
Who can the brave young horseman be?

He is wild but he is mellow.
He is strong but he is weak.
He is cruel but he is gentle.
He is wise but he is meek.

Gordon Lightfoot

IF A TREE FALLS

rain forest
mist and mystery
teeming green
green brain facing lobotomy
climate control centre for the world
ancient cord of coexistence
hacked by parasitic greedhead scam —
from Sarawak to Amazonas
Costa Rica to mangy B.C hills —
cortege rhythm of falling timber

What kind of currency grows in these new deserts,
these brand new flood plains?

If a tree falls in the forest does anybody hear?
If a tree falls in the forest does anybody hear?
Anybody hear the forest fall?

Cut and move on
Cut and move on
take out trees
take out wildlife at a rate of a species every
single day
take out people who've lived with this for 100,000
years —
inject a billion burgers worth of beef —
grain eaters — methane dispensers —

through thinning ozone
waves fall on wrinkled earth —
gravity, light, ancient refuse of stars
speak of a drowning —
but this, this is something other
busy monster eats dark holes in the spirit world
where wild things have to go
to disappear
forever

If a tree falls in the forest, does anybody hear?
If a tree falls in the forest, does anybody hear?
Anybody hear the forest fall?

Bruce Cockburn

ANTHEM

The birds they sang
at the break of day
Start again,
I heard them say
Don't dwell on what
has passed away
or what is yet to be.

The wars they will
be fought again
The holy dove
be caught again
bought and sold
and bought again;
the dove is never free.

Ring the bells that still can ring.
Forget your perfect offering.
There is a crack in everything.
That's how the light gets in.

We asked for signs
the signs were sent:
the birth betrayed
the marriage spent;
the widowhood
of every government—
signs for all to see.

Can't run no more
with the lawless crowd
while the killers in high places
say their prayers out loud.
But they've summoned up
a thundercloud
They're going to hear from me.

Ring the bells that still can ring.
Forget your perfect offering.
There is a crack in everything.
That's how the light gets in.

You can add up the parts
but you won't have the sum
You can strike up the march,
there is no drum.
Every heart
to love will come
but like a refugee.

Ring the bells that still can ring.
Forget your perfect offering.
There is a crack in everything.
That's how the light gets in.

Leonard Cohen

RÉGINE

Sister Régine was the pretty one
She never was lonely for long
And I was poor Ellen the plain one
who never did anything wrong.

Our mother died when we were both young
and I learned to cook and to clean.
Father died slowly of cancer and care
and always he talked of Régine.

CHORUS:
Régine walks like a queen,
loves like a child, lives in a dream.
Régine. What have you done?
You took all the love and left me with none.

Régine left the farm at seventeen,
she had children with two different men
and as she bore them, she brought them to me
and I was a mother to them.

I was near thirty when I married Carl
and I know that he married the land.
But he's steady and he's kind and he's good to the girls
and I know the place needed a man

CHORUS

My sister's two daughters are like night and day
and my heart is caught in between
for one of them's pretty and one of them's plain
and the pretty one looks like Régine.

For sister Régine was the pretty one
who carried herself like a queen;
and I am poor Ellen the plain one
who wishes that she were Régine.

Sylvia Tyson

FLYING ON YOUR OWN

You were never more strong girl
You were never more alone
Once there was two, now there's
    just you
You're flying on your own

You were never more happy girl
You were never oh so blue
Once heartaches begin, nobody
    wins
You're flying on your own

And when you know the wings you
    ride
Can keep you in the sky
There isn't anyone holding back
    you
First you stumble, then you fall
You reach out and you fly
There isn't anything that you can't
    do

You were never more wise girl
You were never more a fool
Once you break through
It's all up to you
You're flying on your own

You were never more together
You were never more apart
Once pieces of you were all that
    you knew
You're flying on your own

Rita MacNeil

COD LIVER OIL
(This version is attributed to Michael Aylward)

I'm a young married man and I'm tired of life,
Ten years I've been wed to a pale sickly wife,
She has nothing to do only sit down and cry,
Praying, oh praying to God she would die.

A friend of my own came to see me one day,
He told me my wife she was pining away;
He afterwards told me that she would get strong,
If I'd get a bottle from dear Doctor John.

Oh Doctor, oh Doctor, oh dear Doctor John,
Your cod-liver oil is so pure and so strong;
I'm afraid of my life I'll go down in the soil,
If my wife don't stop drinking your cod-liver oil.

I bought her a bottle just for to try,
The way that she drank it I thought she would die,
I bought her another, it vanished the same,
And then she took cod-liver oil on the brain.

I bought her another she drank it no doubt,
And then she began to get terrible stout,
And when she got stout of course she got strong,
And then I got jealous of dear Doctor John.

Oh Doctor, oh Doctor, oh dear Doctor John,
Your cod-liver oil is so pure and so strong,
I'm afraid of my life I'll go down in the soil,
If my wife don't stop drinking your cod-liver oil.

Our house it resembled a big doctor's shop,
It was covered with bottles from bottom to top,
And early in the morning when the kettle do boil,
You'd swear it was singin' of cod-liver oil.

This Irish ditty was very popular in the latter part of the nineteenth century and was often heard on the stage. It appeared in several song books of the period including James Larkins Variety Songster, James O'Neil's Emerald Echoes, *and Peter J. Downey's* Let the Poor Go Down. *Its popularity in Newfoundland has led many to suppose that it originated there. It is, however, the sort of comical ditty that so many later Newfoundland ditties are patterned after.*

THE BLACKFLY SONG

'Twas early in the spring when I decide to go
For to work up in the woods in North Ontario,
And the unemployment office said they'd send me through
To the little Abitibi with the survey crew.

CHORUS:
And the blackflies the little blackflies
Always the blackfly no matter where you go.
I'll die with the blackfly a picking my bones
In North Ontario, In North Ontario.

Now the man Black Toby was the captain of the crew,
And he said, "I'm gonna tell you boys what we're gonna do.
They want to build a power dam and we must find a way
For to make the little Ab flow around the other way.

CHORUS

So we survey to the east and we survey to the west,
And we couldn't make our minds up how to do it best.
"Little Ab, little Ab, what shall I do?
For I'm all but goin' crazy on the survey crew."

CHORUS

It was blackfly, blackfly everywhere.
A-crawlin' in your whiskers, a-crawlin' in your hair;
A-swimmin' in the soup, and a-swimming' in the tea;
Oh the devil take the blackfly and let me be.

CHORUS

Black Toby fell to swearin' cause the work went slow,
And the state of our morale was gettin' pretty low.
And the flies swarmed heavy — it was hard to catch a breath,
As you staggered up and down the trail talkin' to yourself.

CHORUS

Now the bull cook's name was Blind River Joe;
If it hadn't been for him we'd never pulled through,
For he bound up our bruises, and he kidded us for fun,
And he lathered us with bacon grease and balsam gum.

CHORUS

At last the job was over: Black Toby said: "We're through
With the little Abitibi and the survey crew."
'Twas a wonderful experience and this I know,
I'll never go again to North Ontario.

CHORUS

Wade Hemsworth

LET ME FISH OFF CAPE ST. MARY'S

Take me back to my western boat,
Let me fish off Cape St. Mary's
Where the hag downs sail and the fog horns wail
With my friends the Browns and the Cleary's.
Let me fish off Cape St. Mary's.

Let me feel my dory lift
To the broad Atlantic combers
Where the tide rips swirl and the wild ducks whirl
Where Old Neptune calls the numbers
'Neath the broad Atlantic combers...

Let me sail up Golden Bay
With my oilskins all a'streamin'...
From the thunder squall—when I hauled me trawl
And my old Cape Ann a'gleamin'
With my oilskins all a'streamin'...

Let me view that rugged shore,
Where the beach is all a'glisten
With the caplin spawn where from dusk to dawn
You bait your trawl and listen
To the undertow a'hissin'.

When I reach that last big shoal
Where the ground swells break asunder,
Where the wild sands roll to the surges toll.
Let me be a man and take it
When my dory fails to make it.

Take me back to that snug green cove
Where the seas roll up their thunder.
There let me rest in the earth's cool breast
Where the stars shine out their wonder —
And the seas roll up their thunder.

Otto P. Kelland

Students and Others

MASQUERADE

He hides behind a mask of
indifference, feigning joviality at
every turn.

He feeds upon the misfortune of
others, to draw attention away from
his own.

He wears many disguises to conceal
the truth that lies heavily in his
heart. The secret that strives so
vainly to be free from the prison
that is his soul.

He is lonely.

Jason Kelly

ONE DAY

I look at her from afar, across a
wide chasm of insecurity. I have
no way to reach her, for that
endless barrier stretches as far
as the eye can see.

Maybe one day, however, I will
learn to fly.

Jason Kelly

ALL I NEED IS SOME...

In the doctor's office
lies the sleek new magazine
beckoning, calling.

Begging for the looks
The attention of passersby
Designed to entrance.

The cover crackles
as I bend it back and see
perfection plastered

From top to bottom
in very gleaming inch
Irresistible

Wafer thin models
prancing, pouting, flirting, toss
silken manes of hair

over shoulder soft
nails lacquered, gleaming
eyes like blue crystal

swept with powdered color
lashes alluring
fluttering like fans

Lips stained with ruby red
full, sensuously curving
over pearl-like teeth

In mid thought I pause
I could be this beautiful
All I need is some...

Suddenly my hands
Red and chapped, nails uneven
Mock my silly dream

I stumble away
from the office—oh, I never
knew my jeans had holes.

Evette Signarowski

LIFE

She sweeps across the floor
A dancer to her own music.
Her steps graceful and sure,
She takes on the world.

A black shape appears
enticed by her movements,
In numbers they grow,
veils of people
to witness the success of their kind.

A stumble; she falls.
Disappointments crawls across her visage.
A shadow steps from the mass
and puts forth a hesitant hand.
She defiantly turns her head.

Pausing only a moment,
She moves one foot.
Slowly, eyes tightly closed
She commences her inert rebirth—
A bud in a garden of weeds.

Triumphantly, her head turns upward
a smile touching her lips.
The rose has blossomed.

She takes a step
And another
testing her stride—
her ability.

The dancer hears her melody;
Her footfalls confident once more,
And the crowd grows...

Kimberly Russell

UNTITLED

Lest we forget,
How to remember,
A piece of time with
no bearing on my
memory.

A child's innocence,
A man's reality
A child's confusion
A mother's sorrow.

War: a word not even
the keenest of minds
can explain. A battle
of senseless killings
that I am told to
remember.

They told you to die
for your country
die for people who
will never be known
to you and a future
no one can predict.

I'm sorry, but this
will not bring you
back, I can cry
for you, but sadly
this could not help
you either.

All I can do is
sit down and try
to understand,
understand the little
disappointment that
loomed over you all.

Natasha Hart

MY DREAMS

We've all had dreams confuse us
And not knowing what to do
We've woken up in terror
When this ordeal was through.

I fell asleep last November
And thought it was July,
Saw cows sit round our table
And fish fill up the sky.

I swam across our living room
And drank a holiday,
Dessert was my clock radio
And my trophies ran away.

My garbage was sweetly singing
As I turned my hair on "bright,"
My hairspray squirted crazily
As my Reeboks picked a fight.

So Happy Unbirthday everyone
For Christmas day has past,
And I'm a busy zoo keeper
Diving underground at last.

Corrie Bisschop

CANDLE OF HOPE

A
light
of hope
sparks
to
life as my
fresh life
ignites with
yours. The
low flame
in threat
of a short
life. But
we nurture
the small
s p a r k
t h r o u g h
storm and
wind unable
to let it
vanish. The
cold, small
fire, now
growing in
warmth. The
romance has
grown as
our flame
e v o l v e d
from a
f l i c k e r
Our candle in
full blaze is
impossible to
extinguish. The
wind and rain may
approach, but we've
battled against all odds
Letting no one threaten
our flaming love.
But as more troubles
seem to approach
I hope our
bursting flame
will survive the
distance and
storm. Never to
die, forever our
burning candle will stand.

Deneen Spracklin

NEWFOUNDLAND

```
        The
        tree
        scras
        handf
        a l lfr
        omthe
        storm
        ynigh        t, the
       snowblo    wsandthew      ind
      howlsagainstthesea, wave           sgr
      owhigheranddangerincrea            ses
     themightyforces          causethesound
     soffearthenthenewf     oun            dlan
     dstormbeginstodied           o      w
        nafterallitsdisa
                  ster
             iscom
              plete
```

April Winsor

THE THIRTEEN CLOCKS

(Written after reading The Thirteen Clocks *by James Thurber)*

In the castle 13 clocks
Lie frozen without ticks and tocks
And a cold Duke so slowly walks
Anticipating Whisper's knocks.

On his eye there is a patch
He has two legs that do not match
But mention this and you will catch
One swift sword from guggle to zatch.

Now, niece Saralinda is standing by
In this castle up so high
When this minstrel Xingu guy
Decides to give his luck a try.

Decides alone it just won't do
So Golux comes to the rescue
Out jump some varlets who say,"boo"
And drag him off to you know who.

Duke unimpressed as you can tell
That someone wanted niece so swell
Into the dungeon minstrel fell
While princess said, "I wish him well".

(Turns out minstrel all forlorna
Is really the Prince Zorn of Zorna)

The Duke decides to keep him alive
As long as thousand gems arrive
And prince and Golux can contrive
For 13 clocks to then strike five.

Some struggle then in here ensues
The prince still tries to pay his dues
Some elements to surely confuse
To tell the ending I refuse.

The story is not very deep
It doesn't really make me weep
The ending is a little steep
But give the Todal room to gleep.

Anneliese J. Ellis

MY FATHER'S HOUSE

Looking back
I recall lying
On the hard, cold earth
With tears held back
And blood on my face.

My father
Stood before me
Towering with authority,
Fists clenched in anger,
Looking down at me.

He had been drinking,
Wrecked his car.
I had been sleeping
The door locked,
Not expecting him home.

He kicked from outside,
I pulled back the bolt.
Missing the open door,
He fell from the step
Into the dirt below.

Afraid he might be hurt,
I went to help him
Back to a staggering stand,
And he punched me
While I held his other hand.

Blood of his own blood
He caused to bleed.
I felt generations of defiance
Gather within me.
My time had come.

As I rose against him,
He swung again,
Inviting a response.
And I watched him collapse
Like a drunken old man.

I stood above him
Mirroring his former self.
He laughed, then cried,
When I held out my hand
And called him"father."

"Hate the world
Before it can hate you,"
Were his words
Of wisdom and warning.
"We have to—be strong,

Drink, fight, never love."
"Emotions are for the weak."
"Laugh when you are hurt."
"Swallow when you are sick."
"A man must never cry."

He drifted into guilty silence
As I reached for my leather jacket,
My boots and a spare shirt.
Looking—full of knowledge,
I followed the sun
Rising beyond my father's house.

Sebastian

CROSSING

Let the light trickle off your rosy cheeks
and dance in the streets of snow.
Let the snow be your pathway
behind the doors that keep you away.
Lift up the curtains and stare from the window
search for those hidden islands that lie
beyond the door.
Look for the coloured archways that point
toward the sky.
Listen for the sweetened scream of the owl
that echoes toward the moon.
Let your soul unite with the moon
Let its web entangle your mind
paralyzed.
Then let your mind
marry the night.
Take it home
Let it dwell.
And someday, together, you will see the
painted archway,
the moon will light your path,
the door will be unlocked,
and you will follow the snow
beyond the threshold
and emerge…

Susan Blagg

A WALTZ IN THE CEMETERY

I, in my faded scarlet dress,
He, in a threadbare tuxedo of black,
Danced on the compressed earth
In the late hours of the night;
We rose above.

Aromas of moistened soil
And decomposing blossoms
Of sorrow and grief
Encompassed us in our evening frolic.

Whirling and twirling
Amongst the headstones,
Paying no heed to the screaming crosses
Perched carefully to reveal dead religion.

Autumn leaves of brown and red
Spun and swirled beneath our feet;
The barren trees bayed at the moon
Blessed with voices from the living wind.

The dew settled on my dress,
And rested on his tux.
And the weight of it pushed us
Back into our places, beneath
The moss and unseeing moles.

We lost our careless joy,
Our flighty feet,
For the two-step
Is so difficult
Six feet below the evening air.

Tereigh Ewert

FOR EARLE BIRNEY IN ST. JOHN'S

Rangy old poet, loping in
From winter with a carpet-bag
Of records, volumes;

Needing no introduction, gently
Whispering, fluting, every word
Distinct and lingering;

A compass rose
Of winds and harbours,
Longings and curiosities

Unquenched; your beard as crisp as snow,
Your pink and white-wisped skull
Innocent as a babe's again;

Eyes crinkled with experience
— War, and death, and love —
And smiling up at us;

Eighty this year, still trying
Everything on, still stretching out
To mythical dimensions;

Lays of a last
Wandering minstrel, wreathed
In the spring leis of our applause.

Philip Gardner

FISHING 1992

For forty-three years
the roll and slap of the sea
lulled this fisherman to sleep.
Now his floating cradle
is swamped by a westerly wave
with lethal intent.
A desperate grasp
leaves only the stinging Atlantic:
he cannot swim.
Sunshine dulls
as pink buoys flatten and vanish.
Momentary grey
precedes a universe
of silent icy darkness.
Euphoric drowning is a nauseating myth.

A weightless fall reveals another time;
each meter counts a year
of fierce independence
in a remote land.
Cracked and clumsy hands
sculpting a culture
destined for pamphlets
and guided tours:
he must swim.

With the crack of the sea bed,
all becomes clear.
A centuries-old revenant
alone with the fish
is able to swim.
Sensation returns at the surface;
forsaking the cradle
that send him to his cold grave,
he swims for shore.
Each stroke stretching out
his half-century slumber.

Peter J. Walsh

NO CHILD IS AN ISLAND

Soft apprehensive
                    steps,
With pant cuffs raised.

Ankles deep in the puddle,
But way over his head.

A spell of concentration
Breaks into anxious glances,

Searching for mommy
Or the reason he's there.

Peter J. Walsh

POEM

So he kisses her and says the three words he has said
To her everyday for the last six years
And she watches him go down the concrete steps
Before she says the three words forming the question
She has been waiting to ask him for the last six hours;
"You'll be back...?" "Ten" he calls over his shoulder
As he begins to jog
Down their street—past the church—across the toll bridge
Finally arrives, and "—office was renovated over
the weekend, sir, won't be ready 'til the tomorrow—"
His heart sings.
The night is free and will be spent with his wife
And the tiny life that grows within her, he thinks, and jogs
Two years married
Two weeks ago she told him with shy pride
He nears their house when he sees the Other
Striding steadily up the concrete stairs
The Other who loved her before
"But never as much" she assured
"But never again" she swore
He stops breathing a moment and the door opens
And the Other walks inside.
He creeps quietly and quickly up the concrete stairs
And he listens and he hears them speak
Until he can hear no more—only the welcome roar
Of the blood pounding through his ears
So he runs... sprints... flies blindly;

Away from their house—down the street—
From his wife—past the church—
From the tiny growing life that was
In a way
Robbed from him but was also
In a larger way
Never his at all
What did he feel as he climbed the steel rail?
Not afraid
It was beyond the inklings of a fear that existed before
It was now a swiftly forced acceptance of the truth
Eagerness—eager to quench the sudden inferno in his mind?
Perhaps
          Probably
                    Yes

          Rob Riggs

THE GOLDFISH

The Goldfish swims through
The water of its crystalline world
Diving and gliding like a bird in
A liquid sky

I watch this creature;
Its color with a lustre richer
Than any metal could offer

And I wonder if it savours
Each mouthful of food it eats
And every breath it draws through its gills
As it relishes each precious moment
Of its short lived life

Or does it eat, breathe and swim
Bitter at its captivity
Exisiting simply because
It can.

Rob Riggs

UNTITLED

To live a life you need a name
to avoid the silence and the shame.
No one to call for you aloud
another lost face among the crowd
The jewels you offer are kept within.
Masked behind a molded grin.
Not even you know who you are
a child delivered from a cosmic afar.
Teasing you, with cries they taunted
You are the child that no one wanted.

Anna Sprague

PAIN

If
you want to avoid pain
lock yourself in a
cocoon
hide
in the depths of your soul and
never let anyone
inside
safe
is what you'll be
pain will never touch
you
but
imagine the butterfly you
could
become
if you'd only take the chance

Rachel Twigg

POSSESSION

I don't trust you
    when you are near
and I don't trust
    myself either.
You can hear my heart
    beating
and you can use it for
    whatever you will.
My heart is defeated,
    it can't struggle
against your strength
    and power.

Vanessa Colman-Sadd

THE AFRICAN ARROW FROG

In the depths of the idyllic wilderness I lie
in ambush surrounded by glorious vistas,
exquisite plant life, and technicolor sunsets.
          — I am at peace —

My handsome pigmentation encloses me in my
kingdom of heather, floral underbrush.
          — I am virtious —

The sky is heavy with grime. I hear their
impending machines. The tranquility of
the woodland is no more.
          — I am afraid —

The timberland is vanishing. The terror is
setting in. The alarm; The stampede; The
destruction.
          — I am extinct —

Sarah Thornhill

THE DEATH OF A FRIEND

At such a young age,
No one would expect,
At such an age aren't we immortal?
At the very least we should expect it.

It's at this age life is just fulfilling it's promises,
And the mind is so full of wonder, love and dreams.
At this age no one would expect a cold, dark
experience to scar our minds and chip away our mortality.

Now when I see your face,
I realize my fears.

Daniel P. Burry

CAMPING ON THREE POND BARRENS

Perched on a black rock,
I scoop clear, slippery water from the third pond
with an ice-cream bucket.
Under the surface,
pebbles glow like dark jewels,
reflecting the voodoo moon.
I listen to the slapping water
and think poetry.

Breaking branches,
breaking moment,
a creature plunges from the woods
and hits the rock hard,
retching and puking.

For one moment,
I turn to run from that
black heap on the rocks,
convulsing with its
heaving,
and tearing,
and choking,
and spitting.

But then I step toward it,
slipping on vomit,
lift its head,
and look into
the contorted face of a child.

On his feet, he's tiny,
eleven, maybe twelve.
Shivering.
Not wearing a coat.
I put my arms around narrow narrow shoulders.

Other children appear between the trees,
wearing hockey jerseys,
carrying cases of beer too big for them.
Lost their camp,
were going to sleep on the ground.
Too drunk to find their way.

I drag,
finally carry the boy
towards our campsite,
the others trailing.
He's not heavy.

I deliver them to our fire.
More than I thought.
Girls too.
No coats.

The smoke from the campfire
scorches my face,
stings my eyes,
chokes my lungs,
and leaves my back cold.

In the hot glow
I watch unfocussed eyes in unfamiliar faces.
Harsh laughter and curses
rising violently
against the silent solemn wood.
I watch the glint of the passing bottle.

I watch one of the girls, the youngest,
with harsh mascaraed eyes and soft baby lips.
Her face strangely angelic as she warms her little feet.
But even when one of the boys
roughly grabs her wrist,
"You're sleeping in my tent, bitch."
It doesn't seem to matter.
She remains unconcerned, serene,
numb.

I hold my boy, the sick one.
Wrap him in blankets.
Give him water.
His name's Dion.

I beg him to leave with me.
I long to deliver him
to a warm bed.
I imagine his life changed.
I imagine myself a kind vision in his memory.
But he won't leave.
Wants to stay with his friends.

So I leave alone.
Walking through the perverse beauty
of the nighttime woods,
thinking poetry,
and crying.

Kristina Fagan

SELECTED BIOGRAPHIES

Milton Acorn (1923-86)

Milton Acorn was born in Charlottetown, PEI, and at various times, has lived in Vancouver, Toronto, and Montréal. His poetic works include *In Love and Anger*, and *The Island Means Minago*. When his book *I've Tasted My Blood* failed to win the Governor General's Award, a group of fellow poets presented him with the first and only Canadian Poetry Award.

Bert Almon (b. 1943)

Bert Almon was born in Port Arthur, Texas but moved to Canada in 1968. He currently lives in Edmonton. His poetic works include *The Return, Poems for a Nuclear Family*, and *Deep North*.

Margaret Atwood (b. 1939)

Margaret Eleanor Atwood was born in Ottawa, and currently resides in Toronto. Her poetic works include *The Circle Game* and *You Are Happy*, as well as a novel, *The Handmaid's Tale*, which was made into a feature movie starring Robert Duvall. She has been the recipient of numerous awards including the Governor General's Award and the Radcliff Medal.

Winona Baker

Self-described as a little old housewife from Nanaimo, Winona Baker grew up in the Fraser Valley of BC. In July, 1989, she took first place among nearly 40,000 entrants in the world haiku writing contest sponsored by the Japanese Broadcasting Corp.

Earle Birney (b. 1939)

Alfred Earle Birney was born in Calgary, an only son, and was raised in Banff and Creston, BC. He has received a Governor General's Award for each of his two first books, *David and Other Poems*, and *Now is Time*. Other works by Birney include *The Collected Poems of Earle Birney*, and *Copernican Fix*.

Bliss Carman (1861-1929)

Born in Fredericton, NB, Bliss Carman was cousin to Charles G. D. Roberts. His first volume of poetry was so well received, he became known as a major 'Canadian nature mystic,' having his poetry more appreciated in the United States than in Canada. During the last two decades of his life he received many honours including several honourary degrees.

George Elliot Clarke (b. 1960)

George Elliot Clarke was born in Windsor, NS. Now a doctoral candidate at Queen's University, he has worked as an editor, publisher, social worker, researcher, and journalist. He has published two collections of his poetry, *Saltwater Spirituals and Deeper Blues* and *Whylah Falls*.

Fred Cogswell

Born in New Brunswick, Fred Cogswell has taught English at UNB for many years. He founded one of Canada's best-known and respected literary journals, *The Fiddlehead*. He has written in many generes but is best known for his poetry.

Leonard Cohen   (b. 1934)

Leonard Cohen was born in Montréal which he continues to consider his home. The works of Cohen, a well-known singer and song writer, include *The Spice-Box of Earth, The Energy of Slaves*, and *Various Positions*. He has won both Juno and Grammy awards for his recordings as well as the Governor General's Award for his writings.

John Robert Colombo

John Robert Colombo describes himself as poet and editor-at-large. He was born in Kitchener, ON, but has travelled widely in Canada and around the world. He is well-known for making unexpected discoveries of 'the poetic' in the most unexpected places and has published two volumes of these found poems. He has written in other genres and also for magazines, reviews and radio.

Isabella Valancy Crawford   (1850-1887)

Isabella Valancy Crawford was born in Dublin, Ireland, but moved with her family to Canada in 1855. In an attempt to help her family, she began to sell short stories and poetry that she had written. Works by Crawford include *The collected poems of Isabella Valancy Crawford, Fairy Tales of Isabella Valancy Crawford*, and *The Halton Boys: A Story for Boys*.

Mary Dalton

Mary Dalton was born in Lake View, Conception Bay, NF. She currently lives in St. John's where she teaches in the department of English at Memorial University. She has published two books of poetry, *The Time of Icicles* and *Allowing the Light*.

Mary di Michelle

Mary di Michelle was born in Italy and immigrated to Canada in 1955. Her works include *Tree of August, Mimosa and Other Poems*, and *Immune to Gravity*. She has won several awards including the silver medal in the Du Maurier Award for poetry.

Tom Dawe   (b. 1940)

Tom Dawe was born in Long Pond, NF where he lives with his family. His Works include *Hemlock Cove and After, In a Small Cove, A Gommil from Bumble Bee Bight*, and most recently *In Hardy Country*. He has been honoured with several awards including the Elizabeth Burton Poetry Prize.

Chief Dan George

Chief Dan George was born in North Vancouver, a member of the Salish tribe of Tell'lall-watt. He became famous after playing opposite Dustin Hoffman in *Little Big Man*, a role for which he was nominated for an Academy Award. He has published one book of poetry, *My Heart Soars*.

Philip Gardner (b. 1936)

Born in Liverpool, England, Philip Gardner studied English Literature at King's College, Cambridge. He is now a Professor of English at Memorial University of Newfoundland. His latest collections of poetry are *A Wind Returns: Selected Poems 1974-1983* and *Talking to Ghosts: Selected Poems 1983-1992*.

Claire Harris

Currently living in Calgary, Claire Harris is the 1987 multiple winner of the Writer's Guild of Alberta Award and the First Alberta Culture Poetry Prize for her book of poetry *Travelling to Find A Remedy*.

David Helwig (b. 1938)

A poet, playwright, and fiction writer, David Helwig was born in Toronto. He has been a consulting editor for Oberon Press and worked as literary manager and script editor for CBC television.

E. Pauline Johnson (1862-1913)

Born Tekahionwake (the smoky haze of Indian summer) on the Grand River Reserve of the Six Nations Indians, Brantford, ON. A writer of prose and poetry, she travelled extensively for sixteen years, reading and giving recitals. There have been sixteen editions of her poetry collection *Flint and Feather*.

pj johnson (a.k.a. The Raven Lady)

A resident of Whitehorse, YK, pj johnson describes her greatest achievement as 'survival.' She is actively involved in the Yukon writing scene and in the promotion of poetry as storytelling and considers herself a storyteller or 'performance poet.'

Joy Kogawa (b. 1935)

Joy Kogawa, a third generation Japanese-Canadian, was born in Vancouver but currently lives in Toronto. Her works include *The Splintered Moon*, *Woman in the Woods*, and the award winning novel, *Obasan*.

Irving Layton (b. 1912)

Irving Layton was born Isreal Lazorovitch in a Romanian Villiage but immigrated to Montréal with his family at the age of one. Since retiring from York University in 1978, he has returned to Montréal where he continues to live. Layton's works include *The Improved Binoculars*, and *Dance with Desire*, as well as *A Red Carpet for the Sun* which won a Governor General's Award.

Dennis Lee (b. 1939)

Dennis Lee was born and raised in Toronto. His poetic works include *Kingdom of Absence* and *Civil Elegies* for which he won a Governor General's Award. He has also published several books of poetry for children inlcluding *Wiggle to the Laundromat* and *Alligator Pie*.

Wanda Legge

Wanda Legge was born in Corner Brook, NF. A graduate in Sociology, Wanda took courses in creative writing at Sir Wilfred Grenfell College. She describes her writing as straightforward and reflecting her interest in relationships between people.

Kevin Major (b. 1939)

Kevin Major was born in Stephenville, NF, and now lives in St. John's. Among his work are four novels: *Far From Shore* which was honoured with the Canadian Young Adult Book award; *Thirty-Six Exposures*; and *Hold Fast* which has been translated into Danish, French, and German and for which he has won the Canadian Council Award for Children's Literature. His most recent novel is *Eating Between the Lines*.

Eli Mandel (b. 1922)

Born in Estevan, SK, Eli Mandel works as both an editor and poet. His writing, *The Idiot Joy*, won a Governor's General's Award in 1967.

Susan Musgrave (b. 1951)

Susan Musgrave was born in California to Canadian parents and grew up in British Columbia. She has travelled extensively but makes her home on Vancouver Island. Her many books of poetry include *Songs of the Sea-Witch* and *Cocktails at the Mausoleum*.

Alden Nowlan (1933-83)

Alden Nowlan was born in Stanley, NS, From 1963 until his death, he was writer in residence at the University of New Brunswick. Nowlan received numerous awards and metals for his work including the Governor General's Award for *Bread, Wine and Salt*. His other works include *The Things Which Are, Smoked Glass*, and *An Exchange of Gifts: Poems New and Selected*.

C.J. Pettigrew

Carol J. Pettigrew was born and raised in Alberta, but currently lives in Whitehorse, YK. She was, for many years, a partner in her husband's guilding and outfitting business and has spent a great deal of time in the wilderness. Many of her writings in several genres have been published widely in Canada.

Al Pittman (b. 1940)

Al Pittman was born in St. Leonard's, NF and currently lives in Corner Brook. His poetic works include *Seaweed and Rosaries, Through One More Window*, and *Once When I Was Drowning*, and most recently *Dancing in Limbo*. He has been the recipient of several awards including the Stephen Leacock Centenial Award, and the Lydia Campbell Award.

Helen Porter (b. 1930)

Helen Fogwill Porter was born in St. John's, NF, where she continues to live and teach at Memorial University. Her works include *Below the Bridge*, and *january, february, june or july*.

E. J. Pratt (1882-1964)

Born in Western Bay, NF, E.J. Pratt is known best for his epic poems. He studied and taught at the University of Toronto and has received many awards including three Governor General's Awards and a Canada Council Medal for distinction in literature.

Al Purdy

Al Purdy was born in Ontario. In the 1930's, he rode trains to Vancouver where he worked for several years in a mattress factory. He served in the RCAF during WW II. Published first in 1944, he has since published 24 volumes of poetry and written many essays and criticisims for radio and TV.

Charles G. D. Roberts (1860-1943)

Born in Douglas, NB, Charles G. D. Roberts worked as both a poet and an editor within Canada, the United States and Europe. He was awarded the Lorner Pierce Gold Medal of the Royal Society of Canada in 1926 and was knighted in 1935. In 1989 he was elected the only non-American charter member of the National Institute of Arts and Letters.

Duncan Campbell Scott (1862-1947)

Born in Ottawa, Duncan Campbell Scott had to forego university due to financial difficulties but became a very successful civil servant. One post was that of Deputy Superintendent-General of the Department of Indian Affairs. He saw the assimilation and eventual disappearance of native cultures as inevitable. He believed his role was one of easing the process of their assimilation and his poetry is often a celebration of the values of these cultures.

David Solway (b. 1941)

David Solway was born in Montréal. He has worked as a poet as well as a broadcaster and scriptwriter for the CBC. He lives in Greece part-time and teaches in Quebec.

Raymond Souster (b. 1921)

Raymond Holmes Souster was born in Toronto where he continues to reside. His works include *When We Are Young, Lost and Found,* and *Poems of a Snow-Eyed Country.* He has been the recipient of both the Governor General's Award and the Centenial medal.

Peter J. Walsh (b. 1970)

Born in St. John's, Peter J. Walsh is an English student at Memorial University. His poetry has been published in *The Sunday Express* and *Wind in the Night Sky,* an American anthology of poetry.

Enos Watts (b. 1939)

Enos Watts was born in Long Pond, NF, and currently resides with his family in Stephenville where he teaches. Among his works are collections of poetry, *After the Locusts* and *Autumn Vengeance.*

Jim Wong-Chu (b. 1949)

Jim Wong-Chu was born in Hong Kong and immigrated to Canada in 1953, where he eventually settled in Vancouver. He has published one book of poetry, *Chinatown Ghosts.*

David Woods

Born in Trinidad, David Woods immigrated to Canada at the age of twelve. He helped to organize the Black Youth Organization and has served as program director of the Black United Front and the Black Cultural Centre in Nova Scotia. He writes for radio and TV and had acted on stage and on film.

INDEX OF POETS

INDEX OF TITLES

ACKNOWLEDGEMENTS

Every effort has been made to trace the ownership of all copyrighted selections included in this text and to make full acknowledgement for those used. If any copyrighted selection has been used without permission or any error made in permission acknowledgement, it will be corrected in subsequent reprints.

A LECTURE IN ECONOMICS by Bert Almon from *Deep North* (Thistledown Press Ltd., 1984), used with permission.

AFRICVILLE by Maxine Tynes. By kind permission of the author.

ALL I NEED IS SOME by Evette Signarowski. By kind permission of the author.

ALL THERE IS TO KNOW ABOUT ADOLPH EICHMANN by Leonard Cohen. From *Stranger Music* by Leonard Cohen. Used by permission of the Canadian Publishers, McClelland & Stewart, Toronto.

ANTHEM written by Leonard Cohen. Copyright 1992 Leonard Cohen Stranger Music, Inc. Used by Permission. All Rights Reserved.

AT A WOOLCO STORE RECENTLY by Kevin Major. Reprinted with the permission of Sterling Lord Associates (Canada) Ltd., Toronto, Ont.

BLOOD AND WATER by Helen Porter. Reprinted by kind permission of the author.

BONNE ENTENTE by F.R. Scott. From *Collected Poems of F.R. Scott* by F.R. Scott. Used by permission of the Canadian Publishers, McClelland & Stewart, Toronto.

BROKEN ARROW. Words and Music by Robbie Robertson. © 1988 MEDICINE HAT MUSIC. All Rights Controlled and Administered by EMI APRIL MUSIC INC. All Rights Reserved. International Copyright Secured. Used by Permission.

CABIN FEVER by Rodene Zimmer. By kind permission of the author.

CAMPING ON THREE POND BARRENS by Kristina Fagan. By kind permission of the author.

CAN U CALL IT by bill bissett. By kind permission of the author.

CANADIAN RAILROAD TRILOGY by Gordon Lightfoot. © 1967 Warner Bros. Inc. All Rights Reserved. Used by Permission.

CANDLE OF HOPE by Deneen Spracklin. By kind permission of the author.

CROSSING by Susan Blagg. By kind permission of the author.

CROSSING TO BRENTWOOD ON THE MILL BAY FERRY by Susan Musgrave. From *A Man to Marry, A Man to Bury*. Reprinted by kind permission of the author.

DEATH BY DROWNING by Elizabeth Brewster is reprinted from *Selected Poems* by permission of Oberon Press.

DEATH OF A YOUNG SON BY DROWNING from *The Journals of Susanna Moodie* by Margaret Atwood. Copyright © Oxford University Press Canada 1970. Reprinted by permission of Oxford University Press Canada

DON QUIXOTE by Gordon Lightfoot. © 1972 Moose Music Inc. Used by permission.

EENIE MEENIE MYNEE MOE by Luigi Pietro Visentin. By kind permission of the author.

EROSION by E.J. Pratt. Copyright University of Toronto Press Incorporated, 1989. Reprinted by permission of University of Toronto Press Incorporated.

EVERYTHING IS FREE by George Elliott Clarke. From *Whylah Falls*, Polestar Press, Vancouver, BC. Reprinted with permission.

EXPLORER from *Da Capo* (1990) by E.D. Blodgett. Reprinted by permission of NeWest Publishers Ltd., Edmonton, Alberta, Canada.

FISHING 1992 by Peter J. Walsh. By kind permission of the author.

FLYING ON YOUR OWN by Rita MacNeil. Reprinted by permission of Balmur Ltd.

FOR EARLE BIRNEY IN ST. JOHN'S by Philip Gardner. By kind permission of the author.

FOR MUSIA'S GRANDCHILDREN by Irving Layton. From *Wild Peculiar Joy* by Irving Layton. Used by permission of the Canadian Publishers, McClelland & Stewart, Toronto.

FUGITIVE by Danny Griffin. By kind permission of the author.

GRANDFATHER by George Bowering. From *George Bowering Selected Poems: 1961-1992* by George Bowering. Used by permission of the Canadian Publishers, McClelland & Stewart, Toronto.

ON POETRY, LOVE, & DEATH by Des Walsh. By kind permission of the author.

ON SAINT-URBAIN STREET by Milton Acorn. By permission of The Estate of Milton J. R. Acorn, Poet.

ON THE WAY TO THE MISSION by Duncan Campbell Scott. Reproduced with the permission of John G. Aylen, Ottawa, Canada.

ONE DAY by Jason Kelly. By kind permission of the author.

PAIN by Rachel Twigg. By kind permission of the author.

PEPPERMINT ROCK by Tom Dawe. By kind permission of the author.

POEM by Rob Riggs. By kind permission of the author.

POEM FOR MY DAUGHTER by Mary di Michele is reprinted from *Necessary Sugar* by permission of Oberon Press.

POSSESSION by Vanessa Colman-Sadd. By kind permission of the author.

PRECISION by Enos D. Watts.By kind permission of the author.

PROSPECTOR by Patrick Lane. By kind permission of the author.

QUEBEC COUNTRY by Claude Péloquin. From *The Poetry of Modern Quebec*, (Fred Cogswell, editor and translator). Montreal, Que.: Harvest House Ltd., 1976. Reprinted by permission.

RASPBERRY RULES by Myrna Garanis. By kind permission of the author.

RECLAIMING by pj johnson. © pj johnson 1988. By kind permission of the author.

RÉGINE by Sylvia Tyson. Copyright © 1975 Salt Music (Copyright Management Inc.). All rights reserved. International copyright secured. Used by permission.

SAGA OF THE SHIELD by Betty L. Dyck. From *Other Channels: An Anthology of New Canadian Poetry*, The League of Canadian Poets. Used by permission.

SALLY'S SONG by Rose Vaughan of the Rose Vaughan Trio from their album "Sweet Tarragon." Used by permission.

SO THIS IS LOVE by Lorna Crozier. From *Angels of Flesh, Angels of Silence* by Lorna Crozier. Used by permission of the Canadian Publishers, McClelland & Stewart, Toronto.

SOAP BOX PREACHER. Words and Music by Robbie Robertson. © 1991 MEDICINE HAT MUSIC. All Rights Controlled and Administered by EMI APRIL MUSIC INC. All Rights Reserved. International Copyright Secured. Used by Permission.

SOUTHERN BOYS by Kate McGarrigle, Garden Court Music ASCAP. From "Dancer with Bruised Knees" by Kate and Anna McGarrigle. Used by permission.

STELLA FUNERALIA by Luigi Pietro Visentin. By kind permission of the author.

TAXI DISPATCHER JAZZ by Mary Dalton. By kind permission of the author.

THE AFRICAN ARROW FROG by Sarah Thornhill. By kind permission of the author.

THE ANT AND THE ELEPHANT by Dennis Lee. Reprinted by kind permission of the author.

THE BALLAD OF ORTHELLO CLEMENCE by George Elliott Clarke. From *Whylah Falls*, Polestar Press, Vancouver, BC. Reprinted with permission.

THE BLACKFLY SONG. Words and Music by Wade Hemsworth. Copyright © 1957 by Southern Music Publishing Company (Canada) Ltd. Copyright Renewed. International Copyright Secured. ALL RIGHTS RESERVED. Used by Permission.

THE DEATH OF A FRIEND by Daniel P. Burry. By kind permission of the author.

THE DRIVER'S SEAT by Shirley A. Serviss. By kind permission of the author.

THE FORSAKEN by Duncan Campbell Scott. Reproduced with the permission of John G. Aylen, Ottawa, Canada.

THE GOLDFISH by Rob Riggs. By kind permission of the author.

THE HYPOCRITES AND THE POET by David Woods. By kind permission of the author.

THE LANDLADY by P.K. Page. By kind permission of the author.

THE LONELY LAND by A.J.M. Smith. From *Classic Shade* by A.J.M. Smith. Used by permission of the Canadian Publishers, McClelland & Stewart, Toronto.

THE MARY ELLEN CARTER by Stan Rogers. Used by permission of Fogarty's Cove Music, cp 1980. All rights reserved.

THE MURDERER by Wanda Legge. By kind permission of the author.